THE TRIUMPH OF THE PHILISTINES

(150 copies only of this edition were printed
February, 1899)

THE TRIUMPH OF THE PHILISTINES

AND HOW MR. JORGAN PRESERVED THE MORALS
OF MARKET PEWBURY
UNDER VERY TRYING CIRCUMSTANCES

A COMEDY IN THREE ACTS

BY

HENRY ARTHUR JONES

AUTHOR OF

'THE TEMPTER,' 'THE CRUSADERS,' 'THE CASE OF REBELLIOUS SUSAN,' 'THE MIDDLEMAN,' 'THE DANCING GIRL,' 'JUDAH,' 'THE MASQUERADERS,' 'THE LIARS, 'THE ROGUE'S COMEDY,' 'THE PHYSICIAN,' 'THE GOAL,' 'THE MANŒUVRES OF JANE,' 'MICHAEL AND HIS LOST ANGEL,' ETC.

New York
THE MACMILLAN COMPANY
LONDON: MACMILLAN & CO., Ltd.
1899
All rights reserved

COPYRIGHT, 1899
BY THE MACMILLAN COMPANY

Mount Pleasant Printery
J. Horace McFarland Company
Harrisburg, Pa.

M. AUGUSTIN FILON, writing in the *Revue des deux Mondes* of the character of Sally Lebrune, says:

"The study is a brilliant one, and at moments really profound. It is the first time, if I mistake not, that an English dramatist, in introducing a Frenchwoman into his work, has turned out anything more than a collection of mere external peculiarities, tricks of facial expression, and mistakes in pronunciation and in language, and that he has penetrated into the very soul, or at least into the *état d'âme*, of another nation, differentiating it from his own."

PREFACE

I NOTICE, on the rare occasions when I go to church, that I roll aloft the Psalms of David with a livelier and lustier relish than any of my neighbors in the adjacent pews. I wish I could claim that this lyric ecstasy arises from a superfœtation of British godliness within me, swelling me to a proud and just conceit of my superiority to all the sinners around me. But, alas! it comes from no such praiseworthy motive, and is indeed nothing but the natural exaltation of an English dramatist on getting some clue to his countrymen's notions on the subject of morality. For these worshippers who are chanting the songs of a treacherous murderer, a liar, and an adulterer — a man after God's own heart, as the Scriptures say — a treacherous murderer, a liar, and an adulterer, — a royal man for all that, — I say, these good worshippers who are so naïvely employed are the same average English playgoers who in the autumn of 1894 arose in a panic of wrathful zeal for the morality of our stage, and in a series of letters to the *Times* overwhelmed for a year or two the rising school of English drama. And it pleases me more than I can say to hear these same good folks thus sweetly discoursing the songs of the royal murderer, liar, and adulterer, in the same way that it pleases me to see the elders of the Scotch Kirk join in the national memorial to Robert Burns. And so, on the rare occasions when I go to church, I roll aloft these Psalms with a glad heart and a loud voice, for then I get a clue to the essential notions of my countrymen on morality. And what are these notions in reality but an echo of Nature's own voice? Listen to the melodious throb of her incessant gong, drowning all the croaks and hisses of priests and creeds, "Vitality is morality! Morality is vitality! Vitality is morality! Morality is Vitality!"

Fortified by the possession of this clue to the essential notions of my countrymen on morality, and having duly read and pondered the letters in the *Times*, I wrote *The Triumph of the Philistines.* The severe ethical purpose underlying its conception was never perceived, and I may perhaps be allowed to point it out.

I have been constantly accused of preaching in my plays, and have never been able to discover on what foundation this accusation rested. Probably it arose from the fact that for many years I have been reiterating a few very plain, simple rules which will have to be comprehended and acted upon before we can pretend to have anything worthy to be called an English national drama. But there is no more preaching in these rules than there would be if, in a degenerate and degraded condition of carpentry, a carpenter were to give a few simple rules in the art of making honest tables and window-sashes. But it is the habit of the Englishman to sniff for doctrine everywhere.

The late William Morris held Socialist meetings at Kelmscott House on Sunday evenings. A Hammersmith woman with a luminous notion of his peculiar tenets was seen to point out his house to a neighbor, exclaiming at the same time, "There's where the good gentleman lives that's so kind to the poor! And he has a Sunday school every Sunday evening!" With the same luminous notion of what I had been saying about the drama, the accusation of preaching in my plays was continually parroted by criticism, and was at length repeated by the venerable *Quarterly Review*.

Now no right-minded man would dream of assaulting his grandmother. Nor would any right-minded man be guilty of offering an indignity or impertinence to a figure so appealing in its senility, and so protected by immemorial prescriptive right of uttering the wrong word in criticism, as the *Quarterly Review*.

And I hope that, however low I may henceforth be classed as a playright, justice will at least be done to my kindness of heart and my reverent forethought for the aged, as witnessed by the fact that months before the article in the *Quarterly Review* appeared, I studied how to justify it by informing *The Triumph of the Philistines* with the severe ethical purpose I have already mentioned.

Having thus determined to vindicate those who find a didactic purpose in my plays, I cast about me for the most suitable moral to illustrate. Looking round upon my countrymen, upon their smug and banal ideals, their smug and banal ways of living, their smug and banal forms of religion, their smug and banal terror of art, their smug and banal haste to make the best of both worlds, I concluded that the most necessary moral to drive home to Englishmen to-day is the wholesome one contained in a verse of Ecclesiastes, "Be not righteous overmuch: why shouldest thou destroy thyself?" Considering the source of this precept, its authority will hardly be questioned by the mass of my countrymen. The necessity for its rigid enforcement will be equally apparent, I hope.

In my strenuous endeavour to enforce a moral I fear I did not take care to write a good play. But thus it happens when a moral purpose is allowed to get the upper hand in a work of art. In any case, I hope the sacrifice of art to ethics which I have made in the following pages will be duly recognized and placed to my credit. And I trust my natural kindness of heart will not be again called upon to vindicate and shelter those who make the assertion that I preach in my plays. For Mr. George Alexander, who produced *The Triumph of the Philistines* with great beauty and taste and consideration for the author, tells me that he lost a hundred and thirty pounds on the run. Alas! for our gallant effort to enforce upon the English people this excellent moral, "Be not righteous overmuch: why shouldest thou destroy thyself?" H. A. J.

30th December, 1898.

Produced by Mr. George Alexander at the St. James's Theatre, 11th May, 1895.

PERSONS REPRESENTED

SIR VALENTINE FELLOWES.
WILLIE HESSELWOOD.
MR. JORGAN ⎰ of Jorgan and Pote, wholesale boot
MR. POTE ⎱ manufacturers, Market Pewbury.
MR. BLAGG.
MR. MODLIN.
MR. SKEWETT.
MR. WAPES.
MR. CORBY.
THOMAS BLAGG.
WHEELER.
FOOTMEN.

LADY BEAUBOYS.
ALMA SULENY.
MISS ANGELA SOAR.
SALLY LEBRUNE.

The Scene is laid in the Hall at "The Studios," near the town of Market Pewbury, in the present time.

Four months pass between Acts I. and II., and two days pass between Acts II. and III.

The following is a copy of the original play-bill of "The Triumph of the Philistines."

ST. JAMES'S THEATRE.

Sole Lessee and Manager — MR. GEORGE ALEXANDER.

To-night, Saturday, 11th May, 1895, and every evening at 8.30,

THE TRIUMPH OF THE PHILISTINES,

and how Mr. Jorgan preserved the morals of Market Pewbury under very trying circumstances

AN ORIGINAL COMEDY, IN THREE ACTS,

By HENRY ARTHUR JONES

SIR VALENTINE FELLOWES. . .	Mr. George Alexander.
WILLIE HESSELWOOD	Mr. H. V. Esmond.
MR. JORGAN { of Jorgan and Pote, wholesale boot	Mr. Herbert Waring.
MR. POTE { manufacturers, Market Pewbury.	Mr. E. M. Robson.
MR. BLAGG	Mr. Ernest Hendrie.
MR. MODLIN.	Mr. Arthur Royston.
MR. SKEWETT	Mr. James Welch.
MR. WAPES	Mr. H. H. Vincent.
MR. CORBY	Mr. Dunkan Tovey.
THOMAS BLAGG	Master Frank Saker.
WHEELER	Mr. Mark Paton.

LADY BEAUBOYS . . . . Lady Monckton.
ALMA SULENY . . . . Miss Elliott Page.
MISS ANGELA SOAR . . . . . . Miss Blanche Wilmot.
SALLY LEBRUNE . . . . Miss Juliette Nesville.

The scene is laid in the Hall at "The Studios," near the town of Market Pewbury, in the present time.

Four months pass between Acts I. and II., and two days pass between Acts II. and III.

Matinee Sunday next and every Saturday at 3. Doors open at 2.30. Carriages at 4.45.

ACT I

SCENE—THE HALL OF THE STUDIOS NEAR MARKET PEWBURY, a large, irregular apartment converted from an old English manor-house.

At the back is a large, wide old oak staircase leading up to gallery, L. *A handsome oak railing in front of gallery. The old ceiling with rafters. A door at the back of the gallery. Downstairs, a door* R. *leading to the living apartments. Downstairs,* L., *a large, old-fashioned fireplace with looking-glass above it. A doorway,* L., *leading to a little outer hall. A small window by the side of the door. The whole scene is most artistically decorated and furnished, and gives evidence in all its details of the greatest taste and care. An easel, holding a large picture with its back to the audience, stands down stage,* R. *The picture is covered with a holland covering which is removed by pulling a string. A very low, long, easy rocking-chair is down stage,* L. *Old armour, swords, shields, etc., hanging on the staircase and walls.*

Enter LADY BEAUBOYS, L., *shown in by* WHEELER.

LADY B. (*a bright, energetic, aristocratic lady of about fifty-five*). Mrs. Suleny?

WHEELER. Yes, my lady.

LADY B. Will you tell her that Lady Beauboys has brought Sir Valentine Fellowes to see her? (*Exit* WHEELER, R.)

LADY B. (*goes to door,* L.; *calls out*). Val! Val! You mustn't do that in England! Val, you'll shock everybody! Dk! Dk! Dk!

Enter, R., ALMA SULENY, *a very young widow in widow's head-dress.*

LADY B. (*cordially*). My dear! (*Kisses her.*) I've brought Sir Valentine to talk over matters with you before Mr. Jorgan and the town council arrive. But——(*goes back to door,* L.; *calls*) Val! (*Comes back to* ALMA.) You know, dear, he never expected to come into the Pewbury estates, and he hasn't lived in England since he left Oxford ten years ago. And, after having spent so much of his life abroad, you can't imagine what a difficulty I have in persuading him that what it is quite proper to do in France and Italy, it is quite improper to do in England. And he has no idea how particular we are in Market Pewbury!

ALMA (*very bitterly*). We are very particular in Market Pewbury.

LADY B. (*goes to picture, draws the cord, pulls aside the holland covering which hangs over it*). Is this the picture that Mr. Jorgan is making all the fuss about? The Bacchante?

ALMA. Yes; that's the picture. Tell me candidly, do you see anything improper in it?

LADY B. (*after having looked at the picture critically*). Not in the least. But I'm quite sure Mr. Jorgan will.

ALMA. It seems so hard, after all my father's and my husband's lifelong exertions in the cause of English art, that just as we discover a young artist with a touch of real genius,—it seems so hard that Market Pewbury should pounce down upon his picture as improper.

LADY B. How did Market Pewbury come to know anything about it?

ALMA. When the butcher boy brought the meat the other morning he caught sight of it in Willie's studio, and described it to his companions. Mr. Blagg, the butcher, heard of it—I'm ashamed to say there's a large bill owing——

LADY B. (*sympathisingly*). My poor dear! That naturally prejudices Mr. Blagg's art criticism.

ALMA. Yes. He declined to serve us with any more meat, brought the matter before the town council, and now they have decided to call a public meeting and demand the abolition or removal of the studios. What can I do?

Lady B. Don't you think you had better give it up?

Alma. But my father? It seems like deserting him. I promised him I would continue his work.

Lady B. Your late dear father and your late dear husband were two seraphs whom an ironic Providence allowed to flutter in a cold commercial world. But it's useless to affirm seraphic traditions in the face of unpaid butcher's bills. You've kept on the studios — how long?

Alma. Nearly two years.

Lady B. Aren't you nearly tired of playing the seraph? Because, my dear, you aren't a seraph by nature, you know. Once take you out of the seraph business, and you'll make a sensible woman. Better give it up!

Alma. To Mr. Jorgan? Never! I'll stay here and carry out my father's wishes while there's a crust to eat, and a single student left to copy a plaster cast of the antique!

Lady B. (*shrugs her shoulders*). Well, I'm sure Sir Valentine will give you all the help in his power. By the way, what does Mrs. Mowbray say to all this?

ALMA. Mrs. Mowbray left me this morning.

LADY B. And you're here without a companion! How foolish! Don't you know what Market Pewbury will say?

ALMA. What does it matter what Market Pewbury says? Besides, if I wished to do anything wrong, what possible hindrance is there in the presence of a middle-aged companion whom I pay?

LADY B. My dear, it's a very venerable and useful superstition that one woman is perfectly safe if another woman is pretending to look after her. And I won't have such a convenient fiction disturbed. You'll please tell your maid to pack up your things, and you'll come back with me in my carriage. Yes, I insist. (*Goes up to picture again.*) Didn't I catch sight of the original of that picture outside?

ALMA. Yes, she's staying with us at the studios.

LADY B. Who is she?

ALMA. Mademoiselle Lebrune—Sally Lebrune she calls herself.

LADY B. (*anxiously*). Sir Valentine went to look round the grounds, and I fancy——(*goes anxiously to door,* L., *and looks off. A loud burst of laughter from* SIR VALENTINE *and* SALLY LEBRUNE *at door,* L. LADY BEAUBOYS *calls out*). Val! Valentine!

Enter SIR VALENTINE FELLOWES, *about thirty, a thorough Englishman by birth and breeding, with slight traces of Continental manners and dress. He comes in, laughing.*

LADY B. Val, you musn't do that in England.

SIR V. (*stops suddenly*). Musn't I laugh in England?
(*Bows to* ALMA, *who bows in return.*)

LADY B. You were talking to somebody outside.

SIR V. Mayn't I talk to a pretty girl in England?

LADY B. Not when anybody's looking. Let me present you. (*Introduces*) Sir Valentine Fellowes — Mrs. Suleny.

SIR V. I'm delighted to meet you. Will you permit me? (*Takes out memorandum-book.*) I'm making a list of things I musn't do in England. I've already filled ten pages.
(*He is writing.*)

ALMA. This is your first visit to Market Pewbury?

SIR V. Yes. There was a quarrel between my father and his brother. My people lived abroad, so, strange to say, I'd never seen Market Pewbury or the estates till I came to take possession the other day.

ALMA. Don't you find Market Pewbury very peculiar?

Sir V. Peculiar? My late uncle seems to have welcomed into his bonnet every possible bee that buzzed round his benighted old head, and the result is that he has made Market Pewbury a complete hornet's nest for his successor. I've already been pestered for subscriptions to seventeen anti-associations — anti-vaccination, anti-vivisection, anti-national-defence, anti-gambling, anti-drinking, anti-eating, anti-smoking, anti-this, anti-that, anti-the-other, anti-enjoy-yourself-or-let-anybody-else-enjoy-himself-in-any-possible-way. Now I'm not an anti-anythingite.

Alma. And all the Market Pewbury people are anti-everythingites.

Sir V. Let every man do exactly what he pleases, I say, because, when he's doing what he pleases he's doing what Nature tells him to do, and that must be right. Why should I set myself up to be wiser than Nature?

Lady B. My dear Val, take the advice of a very wise old woman, and don't stroke Market Pewbury's wool the wrong way.

Sir V. I don't want to stroke Market Pewbury's wool at all, especially that fellow Jorgan's. What I object to is Market Pewbury stroking my wool. What d'ye think? Two confounded old women — I beg pardon — two extraordinary creatures who had the best possible personal reasons for wishing all the other women in the world to conceal their charms, called on me yesterday and asked me to sign a paper pledging myself to persuade all the ladies of my acquaintance not to wear evening dress.

Lady B. What did you say, Val?

Sir V. I said that I considered ladies' evening dress was a very dangerous thing for a man of my temperament to meddle with. And when I declined to commit myself they said they must report me to Miss Angela Soar. Who is Miss Angela Soar?

Lady B. She's the president of the ladies' anti-evening-dress association. She lives in Market Pewbury.

Sir V. In one of my houses?

Lady B. Yes, she's a tenant of yours.

Sir V. (*with a little chuckle*). That's a comfort. As Miss Soar raises the height of ladies' evening bodices, so up goes Miss Soar's rent.

Lady B. Oh no, it won't! Your uncle gave her a very long lease of her house at a very nominal sum.

Sir V. (*blankly*). What did he do that for?

Lady B. He said she was a pure-minded woman with spasms.

Sir V. (*depressed*). It seems to me that all my tenants are pure-minded people with spasms.

Lady B. Yes, I think that would be a very

good description of Market Pewbury. And as you've got to live there for the best part of your life——

SIR V. (*stops her*). Oh no, my dear aunt. There's a Continental "Bradshaw" lying on my table at the Court.

LADY B. But your duties lie here. (*He shakes his head.*) Yes, Val, we musn't forget that property has duties even if other people forget that it has rights. Take an example by me. I live at Market Pewbury six months of the year, in London three or four, and abroad two or three. And I fall in with whatever manners, morals, habits, and religion belong to the place I'm staying at. I'm the most terrible old hypocrite that ever lived! But you can't imagine what an easy time I have, and how much I'm loved and respected by everybody. Now, when I'm at Market Pewbury I think, "Here are all these excellent shop-keeping people content to lead what appears to me a very dull and stupid life all the week, and a much duller and more stupid life on Sunday, and these excellent people do this in order that I may be supplied with groceries, meat, boots and shoes, dress, jewellery, and all the necessaries and luxuries of life. And if these excellent people enjoy being dull and stupid, why should I wantonly destroy their one pleasure in life? Why should I shock them out of their wits by hinting that there are other joys than reading the "Sunday at Home" and playing the harmonium? No! No! I agree with them all. I subscribe to all their chapels—sparingly. I look in at all their mothers' meetings—for a minute or two. I deal at every shop. When I'm swindled moderately, I wink at it. When I'm swindled *im*moderately, I banter the excellent shopkeeper till he's ashamed of himself. And, above all, I avoid committing myself on any subject. And the upshot is, that though, as you say, Market Pewbury is a hornet's nest, *I* never get stung!

Enter WHEELER, R.

WHEELER. Mr. Jorgan and the town council have arrived, ma'am.

ALMA. Show them in here.

LADY B. No. Let me go and soothe Mr. Jorgan's savage breast before he looks at the Bacchante. Perhaps I might show him round the studios, and—(*suddenly*) there's nothing of a shocking nature in the studios, I hope?

ALMA (*considering*). No, I think not. There's a Venus of Milo.

LADY B. Away with her, the baggage! Anything else?

ALMA. And a cast of Hercules.

LADY B. Cover him up, the rascal!

ALMA (*to* WHEELER). Go to the studios and tell Mr. Hesselwood that Mr. Jorgan is going to look round, and ask him to see that nothing is lying about that could possibly shock Mr. Jorgan. (*Exit* WHEELER.)

SIR V. (*has strolled up to the picture*). By Jove! The little hussy who winked at me!

LADY B. Winked at you! Who did?

SIR V. (*pointing to the picture*). She did! The little hussy outside.

LADY B. (*alarmed, to* ALMA). My dear, who is this young person?

ALMA. She is — a sort of artist's model.

LADY B. And you have her staying in the studios? Is that wise?

ALMA. Willie said it would be such an advantage to him to paint from the life, and I thought it would be better for her to stay here than to go into lodgings, as they are very particular in Market Pewbury.

LADY B. But if she winks at people——

ALMA. I've not seen her winking at anybody. And if she does, it's better for her to wink at somebody here than to wink at somebody in Market Pewbury. (*To* SIR VALENTINE.) I'm afraid you found her very forward.

SIR V. No. No. When modesty is quite out of the question with a woman, I think a becoming forwardness is the next best attraction. (*A laugh from* SALLY *outside.*) I say, aunt, I've quite made up my mind as to the propriety of this picture. So I needn't stop to discuss the matter with Mr. Jorgan.

(*Is going off at door*, L. LADY BEAUBOYS *intercepts him.*)

LADY B. Once for all, will you learn the responsibility of your position? You must not do these things in England. (*Bringing him back.*) What made this young person wink at you.

SIR V. (*slightly glancing at himself*). Well, there may have been some good reason.

LADY B. Did you encourage her?

SIR V. I didn't encourage her *before* she winked, but I did encourage her a little *after*.

(LADY BEAUBOYS *shakes her head at him very sternly as at a bad child.*)

Re-enter WHEELER, R.

WHEELER. Mr. Hesselwood have removed everything of a shocking nature from the studios, ma'am.

LADY B. Then I'll begin Mr. Jorgan's art-education. (*To* SIR VALENTINE.) You're to stay here, Val, and promise to help Mrs. Suleny out of her troubles. (*Goes to the picture.*) Hum!

I'm afraid Mr. Jorgan will draw the line at Bacchantes. (*Exit*, L., *followed by* WHEELER.)

SIR V. (*to* ALMA). Now, Mrs. Suleny, tell me all about these troubles.

ALMA. You've heard of my father's scheme for the education of young artists. It was his idea that a man who is born to be an artist is fit for nothing else.

SIR V. Quite true. And generally he's not fit even for that.

ALMA. So he let it be known amongst all the schoolmasters in the country that if they had any good-for-nothing boys who wouldn't or couldn't do their lessons, but who had a decided talent for drawing, that he would examine their work, and if it showed any promise he'd give them a sound art-training here.

SIR V. Your father must have been a perfect godsend to the schoolmasters. How many boys did you get?

ALMA. We've had about two thousand through our hands.

SIR V. And what has been the result?

ALMA. Some of them are doing well as drawing-masters and painters in a small way. And we've discovered one real genius.

SIR V. The painter of this picture?

(*Pointing to picture.*)

ALMA. Yes. My father always prophesied

he would astonish the world one day. Don't you think he will?

Sir V. (*goes to picture*). I think he'll astonish Market Pewbury! What induced your father to choose this place for his studios?

Alma. The air is so bracing ——

Sir V. It is. (*With a little shiver.*) Just a little too bracing for Bacchantes to frolic about in, eh?

Alma. And your late uncle gave him a long lease of this ramshackle old place at a very low rent; so he rebuilt it, added all the studios, and made the boys thoroughly comfortable.

Sir V. (*looking round*). Yes, I should think the boys have had a good time of it. Did your father find it pay?

Alma. He never thought of money. He thought only of art. Don't you think his scheme was a good one?

Sir V. Excellent! And it seems to have one great advantage over the general run of philanthropic schemes.

Alma. What is that?

Sir V. Your father only lost his own money. Most philanthropists lose other people's.

Alma (*hurt*). I can't get any one to believe in my father's work.

Sir V. My dear Mrs. Suleny, I know very little about art, but so far as I can gather, it's something like religion, a vague, indefinite kind of thing, very much talked about, very little understood, and very rarely practised. How has your father's scheme helped English art?

ALMA. We've discovered a genius.

SIR V. Don't you think he would have discovered himself? It seems to me that the net result of your father's well-meant exertions is some few hundreds of good-for-nothing boys turned into indifferent painters and drawing-masters, and one genuine artist painting Bacchantes for Mr. Jorgan and Market Pewbury to cavil at.

ALMA (*discouraged*). Oh, very well. Then I'd better give it up and let Mr. Jorgan come in and take everything.

SIR V. What has Mr. Jorgan to do with it?

ALMA. I had to borrow money on the lease at the bank, and it seems Mr. Jorgan was the person who advanced it. And as I couldn't pay it back in time, I was obliged to make over the remainder of the lease to him. And this will be the end of my father's work!

(*Breaking down, trying to stop her tears.*)

SIR V. Mrs. Suleny, don't give way.

ALMA. I won't. I'm ashamed for you to see me crying.

SIR V. I assure you I have the greatest respect for your father's work, and I shall consider it my duty to carry out his wishes in the best possible way.

ALMA. Do you really mean that? You're only saying it because you're kind! You're not doing it for the sake of art.

SIR V. Oh yes, I am!

ALMA. Are you sure?

SIR V. Well, chiefly for the sake of art, and a little—a very little, for the sake of a lady in distress.

ALMA. You won't think I've been crying and making a scene only to get your sympathy?

SIR V. I'm sure this (*looking at her tears*) is Nature—not art. Now, about this Jorgan——

ALMA. You don't know how he has persecuted my father and me since we've been at Market Pewbury.

SIR V. Why do you let him come here to-day?

ALMA. The town council sent me a notice that they wished to inspect the picture. How could I refuse without giving them a handle for slandering me all over the country? I went to Lady Beauboys and asked her what I should do. She advised me to send them a very polite invitation to inspect it this afternoon, and she promised, like the dear kind soul that she is, to bring you over to meet them, so that you might throw all your influence on my side. And you were good enough to come.

Sir V. For the sake of art.

Re-enter Lady Beauboys, R.

We won't talk any more about art. You hate this fellow Jorgan and all his crew! So do I. Very well. I'm fond of a fight. We'll fight him, you and I, and we'll see who's master in Market Pewbury, Jorgan or I.

Lady B. He'll beat you, Val. You're fighting the strongest force in English life — that black, bitter, stubborn Puritanism that you'll never change, my dear boy, till you've changed the climate of the country and the very bone and marrow of our English race. Jorgan will beat you, Val.

Sir V. We shall see.

Lady B. (*to* Alma). My dear, Mr. Jorgan wants to inspect the boys' dormitories.

Alma. What for?

Lady B. I don't know, my dear. He was just fishing out a Diana and her Nymphs in the studio, and I had the greatest difficulty in keeping him from inspecting them. I'm sure it will do him more good to inspect a nice plain whitewashed wall, and he'll understand it so much better. Come, my dear, humour him.

ALMA. What will be the next indignity that I shall have to endure from Mr. Jorgan? The boys' dormitories!

(*Exit* ALMA, R. SIR VAL *is strolling up to the picture.* LADY BEAUBOYS *pulls the string and draws the cover over it. Exit* LADY BEAUBOYS *after* ALMA, R. SIR VALENTINE *strolls up to the picture, lifts up the holland cover with his hand without pulling the string.* SALLY LEBRUNE *creeps on very slowly,* L. *She is an impish, black-eyed, French girl, dark complexion, red lips, engaging impudent manners, odd little sly French tricks of gesture and grimace, large gold earrings, and bright tawdry coquettish dress. She creeps very stealthily and slowly on tiptoe behind* SIR VALENTINE, *comes up behind him, bursts into a loud fit of laughter behind his ears. He starts and looks at her.*)

SALLY. That is me. How you like me?
(*Pointing to picture.*)

SIR V. (*approaching her*). You monkey! How dare you!

SALLY. I dare do anything in this blessed

ACT I   THE TRIUMPH OF THE PHILISTINES   19

mortal world. I dare make ugly faces at you. (*Makes an ugly face at him.*) I dare make pretty faces at you. (*Makes a pretty face at him.*) I dare do that at you! (*Suddenly putting her thumb to her nose for a moment.*) I dare do that to all this mortal blessed world.

    (*Putting her thumb to her nose and
     swinging round on her heel.*)

  SIR V. You daren't do that to Market Pewbury!

  SALLY (*snaps her fingers*). That at Market Pewbury! (*Puts out her tongue.*) That at Market Pewbury! What you think of Market Pewbury?

  SIR V. What do you?

  SALLY. I think it is full of dam nonsense!

  SIR V. Hush! You musn't say that!

  SALLY. When something is full of dam nonsense will I not say it is full of dam nonsense?

  SIR V. Not in England.

  SALLY. What will I say then?

  SIR V. You might say it's full of D. N.

  SALLY. D. N.? Ver' well. I will say to Market Pewbury, "Market Pewbury, you are full of D. N. till you bust up yourself."

  SIR V. What do you think Market Pewbury will say to you, and—this?

      (*Pointing to picture.*)

  SALLY. What you think of that picture?

SIR V. Exquisite — as exquisite as you are.

SALLY. I will tell you why. The silly boy who painted that, he is just two millions of foots deep in love with me. He is funny, my poor little fool. I twist him round, round, round (*gesture with her fingers*), and when I wink at him like that (*winking very wickedly at* SIR VALENTINE), it send him cracked out at his senses.

SIR V. (*looks at her*). Yes, I should think it would. (*Suddenly struck with an idea.*) I say — would you ——

SALLY. Would I — yes, I think I would. What would I?

SIR V. Mr. Jorgan is coming to look at your picture. While he is looking at it, do you think you could manage to wink at him like that?

SALLY. Like that? (*Winks at him.*)

SIR V. Yes.

SALLY. How much will you give me?

SIR V. (*taken aback*). Money?

SALLY. Yes, I love money so much, and I never have not a blessed mortal sixpence. You are ver' rich, yes?

SIR. V. Hum ——

SALLY. Oh, I could love to have millions and millions and millions of pounds. I could spend it all. Ah, give me some money! And

ACT I THE TRIUMPH OF THE PHILISTINES   21

I will give Mr. Jorgan some nice winks. Ah! You shall see! He will be funny to look at when I wink at him. Give me some money!

SIR V. (*taking out purse*). Well, I don't mind a five-pound note to see the performance.

SALLY. Oh, do give me ten! Yes! (*Snatching the purse from his hand, running away with it.*) I will have ten——

SIR V. (*running after her*). Give me my purse, you little devil!

(*Catches her from the back round the shoulders, struggling with her to get the purse.* JORGAN *has entered quickly behind* SIR VALENTINE *at the door,* R., *which has been left open by* LADY BEAUBOYS *and* ALMA. *He is followed by* MR. SKEWETT. JORGAN *is a middle-aged man of the better tradesman class in a provincial town; thick-set figure; drab complexion with black speckles all over it; stubby, reddish-brown hair, and a line of stubby, reddish whiskers under chin; a coarsely humorous expression of face, loud, vulgar manners, and loud, vulgar laugh.* SKEWETT *is a little sniffing, rasping man with small, spare, feeble, bent figure; mean, irregular features, badly arranged round a formidable, bent, broken red beak of a nose; thin, straggling gray hair, and long straggling, gray, mutton-chop whiskers; constantly blinking little eyes, and very assertive, energetic manners; a constant air of objecting to everything and everybody on principle. The struggle between* SALLY *and* SIR VALENTINE *goes on, watched by* JORGAN *and* SKEWETT.)

SALLY (*protesting*). No, no, no——
SIR V. Give me my purse.
SALLY. Will it be ten pounds, then?
SIR V. Oh, very well, say ten pounds, and be quick about it.
JOR. (*coming a little forward*). Ten pounds, Sir Valentine! Did you hear that, Mr. Skewett?
SKEW. (*in a quick, rasping, nervous, quarrelsome tone*). Yes, I did, and it requires explanation.

(*With a ferocious nod and wink at* SIR VALENTINE.)

Enter LADY BEAUBOYS *and* ALMA, *followed by* MR. WAPES, MR. BLAGG, MR. CORBY, MR. MODLIN, *and* MR. POTE.

MR. WAPES *is a large, flabby, sleepy man, with a rolling walk, bandy legs, no neck to speak of; a body and head all in one piece, shaped like a pyramid, his bald head forming the polished apex, and his large, flabby cheeks fitting loosely over his shoulders; a very weak, wheezy, crackling voice.*

MR. BLAGG *is a stubborn, earnest man; black, shiny clothes; a large, clean-shaven face, and coal-black hair; very solemn manner; twangy, ranting utterance, accompanied by one stereotyped emphatic gesture of a local preacher, his fists closed, and his arms moving mechanically up and down, his body swaying to and fro meanwhile.*

MR. CORBY *is a little, merry-eyed, apple-faced man, with ginger whiskers and bright red hair; a little snub nose; good-humoured features, expressing great general satisfaction with himself and the universe for no particular reason; a short, round little figure; a disposition to giggle and snigger all through the interview.*

MR. MODLIN *is a very long, loosely-built man, with pale complexion, colourless lips, colourless drab hair; vague, irregular features, with entire absence of expression; keeps his hands folded one over the other at full length in front of him, and his eyes fixed in a corner of the ceiling with utter absence of expression.*

MR. POTE *is a meek, mangy, smirking little man, with the most offensive amiability of manner, and a habit of affectionately stroking the person he is talking to; weak, watery eyes; hair carefully pomatumed into a triangle on the top of his forehead; walks on tiptoe, bobbing up and down as if he were afraid of giving offense by too great self-assertion in walking in the ordinary way. They follow* LADY BEAUBOYS *one at a time, take up different positions and look round in a generally embarrassed and ill-at-ease manner.*

LADY B. Now before we look at the picture, I'm sure, Sir Valentine, you will be delighted to make the acquaintance of some of your neighbors at Market Pewbury. (*Introducing.*) Mr. Wapes. (*Bow between* WAPES *and* SIR VALENTINE.) Mr. Modlin, Mr. Corby, Mr. Pote, Mr. Blagg, Mr. Skewett. (*As she introduces them, each of them gives a bow in his peculiar manner.*) I think you already know Mr. Jorgan.

JOR. (*with a laugh*). No, I don't think he does. I take a great deal of knowing, and the more some people know me, the less they like me. (*Rubbing his hands cordially.*) Ha! Ha! Curious taste on their part, isn't it?

SIR V. How curious?

(LADY BEAUBOYS *makes signs to* SIR VALENTINE.)

JOR. Well, Sir Valentine, perhaps the more *you* know of me the less *you'll* like me!

SIR V. (*amused*). I think it not improbable. But I don't intend to know you very well.

JOR. (*cordially*). Oh yes, you will, Sir Valentine, before you're very much older. (*Glancing round for approval at the others.* SKEWETT *nods and blinks viciously.*) Now, as you're the chief owner of property in Market Pewbury, we expect you to set us a pattern.

SIR V. A pattern of what?

JOR. A pattern of moral respectability.

SIR V. Pray don't? Surely property has burdens enough without having to pretend to be better than all it's neighbours. Oh no, Mr. Jorgan! Take it out of me in rates and taxes!

JOR. (*rubbing his hands cordially, and glancing round to his comrades for approval*). Well, I daresay you'll find us equal to that! But first of all, I want to ask you in the nicest and politest way possible, what is the benevolent institution which you were contributing to when I came into the room?

(SKEWETT *pushes forward and nods and*

blinks venomously at SIR VALENTINE *all through the interview. He gives a nod of approval every time anything is said of which he approves.*)

SIR V. Benevolent institution?

JOR. You were about to subscribe ten pounds to this female.

(*Turns suddenly round on* SALLY.)

SALLY (*shrieks*). Female! Ha! What is female? He call me female!

JOR. (*sternly to* SALLY). Female! (*To* SIR VALENTINE.) It must have been for some very benevolent purpose that you gave your purse to this (SALLY *looks very fiercely at him*)—young person. (SALLY *looks a little mollified.*) She has it in her hand now!

(*Pointing at* SIR VALENTINE'S *purse in* SALLY'S *hand.* LADY BEAUBOYS *and* ALMA *show surprise and vexation.*)

SIR V. (*to* SALLY). Will you give me my purse, please?

SALLY. Ah, but you promised——

SIR V. My purse, please! (*Very sharply.*)

SALLY. Ver' well. (*Giving him the purse.*) Ten pounds if you please.

(*Holds out her hand.* SIR VALENTINE *takes the purse.*)

SIR V. Thank you. (*Opens it, takes out a bundle of notes, takes two of them, puts the rest*

ACT I   THE TRIUMPH OF THE PHILISTINES   27

back in the purse, puts his purse in his pocket, turns to JORGAN.) You wish to know why I am giving ten pounds to this young lady?

JOR. You needn't inform against yourself unless you like.

SIR V. I won't. It is for a very good purpose which we will keep to ourselves.

(*Gives two notes to* SALLY.)

SALLY. Ah! Thank you.

    (*Slightly winks at him. Surprise and great consternation on the part of all assembled. Group breaks up.* LADY BEAUBOYS *shakes her head, and shows surprise and vexation.*)

SIR V. And now, gentlemen, if Mrs. Suleny will allow us, we will take your opinion on this work of art.

ALMA. Sir Valentine, oughtn't the artist to be present while his picture is criticised?

SIR V. Certainly. (ALMA *rings bell.*) It cannot fail to be instructive to him to hear these gentlemen's views.

    (SALLY *gets up to* JORGAN, *and, unnoticed by all the others, winks very slyly and wickedly at him. He shows great surprise, horror, and indignation, and moves away from her for a moment. She follows him, does this all through the interview.*)

Enter WHEELER, R.

WHEELER. Miss Soar is outside, ma'am, and says she must come in.

ALMA (*resignedly shrugs her shoulders*). By all means. Show Miss Soar in, and ask Mr. Hesselwood if he will kindly come here.

>(WHEELER *stands back a step to let* MISS SOAR *pass him. Announces* "*Miss Soar.*")

Enter, R., MISS SOAR, *a maiden lady of about thirty-five, very nervous and delicate-looking, in a very plain dress, with a very high collar all round the neck, a pale, sharp face, features drawn into an expression of pained earnestness. She enters hurriedly, panting, one hand on chest, the other carrying a bundle of pamphlets.*

MISS SOAR (*excitedly*). Am I in time? (*Gives a pamphlet to* LADY BEAUBOYS.) Am I in time? (*Gives a pamphlet to* ALMA, *goes up to* SIR VALENTINE.) Am I in time to make my voice heard?

SIR V. (*soothingly*). My dear, lady I believe so. Take a seat. (*Gets her seated. She sits down out of breath.*) On what particular subject would you like to address us?

MISS SOAR. There is but one subject that concerns the women of England to-day.

SIR V. Dress, I should say?

MISS SOAR. Yes. Read that. (*Forcing a pamphlet into his hand.*) I cannot tell you how it shocks me to discuss these subjects with those of the opposite sex.

SIR V. Very well, my dear lady, don't do it, don't do it! For I assure you it shocks us quite as much.

MISS SOAR (*hand on chest, breathing painfully*). And I suffer constantly from spasms——

SIR V. Very well, my dear lady, stop at home and attend to them.

MISS SOAR. How can I? How can I rest, how can any modest woman rest, how can any modest man rest, while thousands of our countrywomen are wearing evening dresses every evening.

SIR V. Well, they must wear something. What do you propose for evening wear?

MISS SOAR. A simple gown, fastened tightly round the neck.

SIR V. Something like the one you are wearing now?

MISS SOAR. Yes. Excuse me (*hand on chest*), I have a slight spasm.

SIR V. (*sympathetically*). Perhaps a little loosening of the neckband——

MISS SOAR (*horrified*). Oh no, please! I'm better now. Promise me you'll read that (*alluding to pamphlet in his hand*), and never rest till our legislature has made it impossible for English women to insult themselves by wearing low-necked dresses.

SIR V. What, all English women?

MISS SOAR. Yes, all.

SIR V. No! No! But I don't mind a compromise. Ladies over forty to submit to your regulations. Ladies under forty to do as they please.

(SALLY *again comes up to* JORGAN, *and, unnoticed by the others, slyly winks at him. He looks at her again with somewhat less indignation than before, and moves away.*)

JORGAN (*moving away from* SALLY). Come! Isn't it time we had a peep at this classical masterpiece?

MISS SOAR. Oh, Mr. Jorgan, if there is anything in it that would shock any modest woman, or any modest man, why look at it at all?

SKEW. (*blinking viciously*). Just so! Burn it, I say! Burn it, and have done with the iniquity.

WAPES (*in a slow, wheezy voice*). No, I shouldn't say burn it. I should say lock it up somewhere where it can't be seen, eh, Mr. Modlin?

Mod. (*vaguely looking at the ceiling*). Yes, in a damp room.

Alma. Don't you think you may as well look at the picture before you condemn it?

Miss Soar. Oh, do not let us run any risk. Oh, how can people be so wicked? I'm sure, Mr. Pote, you agree with me.

Pote (*meekly, bobbing up and down*). Yes, let us ask ourselves what will be conducive to the interests of morality. I always do all I can to help on morality. That's my rule in life, and I do wish everybody would follow it.

Lady B. Oh, Mr. Pote, this is a very moral picture, quite calculated to promote the best and soundest morality amongst the masses, I assure you. And when the artist comes he will be able to show you its beauties.

Blagg (*in a measured, solemn twang, his body swaying to and fro, his arms repeating his one mechanical gesture*). We ain't here to inquire into its beauties, Lady Beauboys. (Skewett *nods and blinks*). We are here to ask our consciences this solemn question, is it a elevating exhibition for my boy Thomas when he brings the jints of a morning? Likewise what will be the momentious effects in after life on the grocer's boy if he happens to catch sight of it? Likewise the baker? Likewise the greengrocer?

Sir V. And the milkman, Mr. Blagg. Don't forget that the milkman has morals that require constantly looking after.

Blagg (*very aggressively*). Likewise the milkman. (Skewett *nods and blinks.*)

Sir V. And your boy Thomas, where is he?

Blagg (*same aggressive tone*). My boy Thomas is employed in the minding of my horse and gig in the yard at the back of this house.

Sir V. We'll have him in. Mrs. Suleny, the butcher boy's morals are at stake. He ought to be here!

Alma (*ringing the bell*). Oh, by all means bring in the butcher boy!

> (Sally *has again sauntered after* Jorgan. *She passes by him, nudges him with her elbow as if by accident, winks at him unnoticed by the others.* Jorgan *again starts, shows less surprise, less horror, less indignation, cannot understand it, glances at her questioningly for an explanation; she again winks, he pulls himself together, looks at her very sternly. Meantime* Wheeler *enters,* R. Alma *speaks to him in dumb show.*)

Alma (*to* Wheeler, *at conclusion of* Jorgan's *business with* Sally). Yes, bring him in.

(*Looking off.*) And here comes the artist himself.

Enter, R., WILLIE HESSELWOOD, *a bright, eager young fellow of twenty-five.*

ALMA (*introducing*). Sir Valentine, may I present Mr. Willie Hesselwood? (*They bow.*) Willie, these gentlemen are now ready to inspect your picture.

WILLIE (*dubiously*). Delighted, but (*looking at them*) I'm sure they won't understand it.

LADY B. Oh, I'm sure they will — when you've explained it to them.

MISS SOAR (*suddenly*). Oh, it is so wrong to be present. I feel I cannot stay!

SIR V. Very well, my dear lady, don't! Run away! Run away!

MISS SOAR. I must — and ——
    (*Puts her hand suddenly on chest.* POTE *comes up to her sympathisingly.*)

POTE. Spasms again? (*Gives her his arm, leads her out.*) Gentlemen, if you please. Miss Soar has spasms! If you please! (*In a confidential aside to the group as he passes.*) Spasms! Spasms!
    (*Takes her off very officiously and tenderly,* L., *walking on tiptoe up and down.*)

D

Enter WHEELER, R.

WHEELER (*announcing*). Thomas Blagg.

THOMAS BLAGG, *a boy of about fourteen, enters very uncomfortably, self-conscious, glancing round nervously, evidently very much afraid of his father; he is approaching the centre of stage.*

BLAGG (*sternly*). Thomas, you stand where you be, and you behave yourself.
> (*Stands* THOMAS *face to audience with his back to easel, where he remains all the while.*)

THOMAS. Yes, father.
> (*Cap in hand, stands at attention, meets his father's eye, shifts about uncomfortably, all through the interview.*)

SIR V. (*solemnly*). One word, Thomas Blagg, you have seen the picture on that frame?
> (THOMAS *glances very nervously at his father, looks very uncomfortable.*)

BLAGG (*sternly*). Can't you speak?

THOMAS. Yes, father.

SIR V. And when you saw the picture, Thomas, what did you say?

THOMAS. What be I to say, father?

BLAGG. Speak the truth for once, if you can.

THOMAS. I says——

(*Pause—looks nervously at his father.*)

BLAGG. The whole truth and nothing but the truth, you young liar. Now? What did you say?

THOMAS (*nervously*). I says — I says — I says —"Oh, crikey and Jeeroosalem, ain't she a jolly stunner!"

(BLAGG *threatens* THOMAS *in dumb show.*
SALLY *has again followed* JORGAN, *who turns round to* WILLIE.)

JOR. (*impatiently*). Now, Mr. Artist, will you show us your picture? What do you call it?

WILLIE. A Bacchante.

JOR. A Bacchante? What's that? A sort of female Bacchus, eh?

SALLY. Female! Ha!

WILLIE. Well, not precisely — but perhaps that's near enough.

JOR. Oh no, it isn't. Mr. Skewett, you're an apostle of temperance——

SKEW. (*blinking*). Yes. And I want a plain answer to a plain question. Is this picture a female Bacchus, or is she not?

WILLIE (*drawing the cord, and flinging off the cover*). Gentlemen, she is just whatever you please! Say what you choose of her. She'll make no reply.

(*Laughs at them, goes upstairs at back*

and sits up there apart the rest of the interview. JORGAN *is standing back, he presses a step forward, looks at the picture, and then looks at* SALLY *surprised.*)

SALLY (*to* JORGAN). That is me!

(*Goes and stands apart from him.* JORGAN *follows her with his eyes furtively every now and then. The others come up to the picture in a group, look at it, look at each other.* CORBY *has a fit of involuntary tittering which he checks under* BLAGG'S *solemn frown, looks in his hat. The others look perplexed, uncomfortable, shocked, stand round and stare at each other.*)

SIR V. Well, gentlemen?

WAPES. Outrageous! Outrageous and audacious I call it!

MOD. Ain't fit to be seen by respectable people.

SKEW. Burn it! Burn it!

(*Blinking energetically.*)

BLAGG. Are we living in heathen Greece and Rome, or is this Market Pewbury? (*Shakes his fist threateningly at* THOMAS.) Oh, Thomas!

(THOMAS *begins to cry.*)

WAPES. Shocking to a degree!

SIR V. Shocking to what degree, Mr. Wapes?

WAPES. Shocking to that degree as Mrs. Wapes wouldn't have it in our drawing-room.

SIR V. Ah, you think Mrs. Wapes would object. (*Turning to* MODLIN.) And what would Mrs. Modlin say?

MOD. Mrs. Modlin would blush to have an opinion on such a matter.

SIR V. (*turning to* BLAGG). And Mrs. Blagg?

BLAGG (*very aggressively*). Mrs. Blagg is my property I believe, not yours!

SIR V. Is Mrs. Blagg the stout lady in the green dress whom I saw at the shop door?

BLAGG. She is.

SIR V. (*emphatically*). She is your property, not mine! And may I ask what Mrs. Skewett would say? (*Indicating picture.*)

SKEW. Before Mrs. Skewett went to glory she had precisely the same opinions on every subject that I had. I took care of Mrs. Skewett's opinions.

SIR V. (*aside to* ALMA). She'd change them the first chance she'd got.

Re-enter POTE, L., *with his tiptoe walk.*

POTE. I've attended to Miss Soar's spasms, and now perhaps I may be permitted to see the picture.

Sir V. Certainly. This way, Mr. Pote.
(POTE *goes up to the picture.*)

POTE. Oh dear! Oh dear! It cannot be considered as conducive to the interests of morality, can it?

SIR V. (*to* CORBY). And you, sir, what do you think of the picture?

CORBY (*nervously, with an inclination to titter*). Well, I was just saying to Mr. Wapes that I really don't see as she's so very bad — not if she had a little more on round her neck — and so forth.

LADY B. Well, that can be easily managed. Mr. Hesselwood, can't you put a few more frills on your Bacchante? Just a little lace, or something, eh?

WILLIE. I won't change a rag, or a ribbon, or a button of her to save an empire from perdition! She's as perfect as I can make her.

SIR V. Now, gentlemen, you've all seen the picture, have you made up your minds?

SKEW. Yes, we have made up our minds.

BLAGG. Likewise the minds of our wives, likewise our daughters, likewise our sons.
(*Threatens* THOMAS *very severely.*)

SIR V. I can quite understand that the ladies of Market Pewbury may for personal reasons object to any outside standard of feminine perfection being placed before the eyes of their husbands. I can also understand, judging from Mr. Blagg's proud assertion of his possession of Mrs. Blagg, that Market Pewbury has not quite the same standard of feminine perfection as heathen Greece and Rome. It seems to me that the matter is capable of being settled in a way that will be very agreeable to all concerned. Those of you who are shocked and find their feelings and their morals hurt by looking at the picture, please to hold up your hands.

(BLAGG, MODLIN, SKEWETT, POTE, WAPES *put up their hands decidedly.* CORBY *puts his up a little way very undecidedly.* JORGAN *is about to put his up,* SALLY *passes by him and jogs his elbow. He puts up both hands instantly.*)

SIR V. Please to keep your hands up. Now! You're all quite sure that you're shocked by this picture?

(*Chorus of "Yes, yes, yes."*)

SIR V. It rouses evil thoughts in your breasts?

(*Chorus of "Yes, yes, yes,"* JORGAN *looking at* SALLY.)

SIR V. Very well. Then if I were you I wouldn't look at it. On the other hand, those of us whose morals and feelings are more robust, ought, I think, to be allowed to look at it as much and as often as we please.

(*Going up to it, looking at it with evident admiration.*)

JOR. Oh no, Sir Valentine, we aren't going to allow you privileges that we deny to ourselves.

SIR V. You're going to look after my morals as well as your own?

JOR. Well, we fancy that your morals want a lot of looking after. Of course, we shall be delighted to find that we're mistaken. Gentlemen, I shall call a public meeting of our fellow-townsmen, and move that this picture is harmful to the morals of Market Pewbury, and I shall demand its instant destruction.

SIR V. Mr. Hesselwood, is this picture for sale?

WILLIE. If any one will buy it, and will let me paint another like it, or (*glancing at* SALLY) a lovelier one, if I can.

SIR V. What's the price?

WILLIE. Well, I don't know. Two hundred pounds? A hundred?

SIR V. I'll post you a cheque for two hundred pounds to-night, and I'll send for it as soon as I get back to the Court.

JOR. You've bought the picture?

SIR. V. I've bought the picture.

JOR. I shall be obliged to mention that at the public meeting. And also to demand its instant removal, and the instant removal of this——

SALLY. Ah, I will not be a female. If you call me that, I will call you—I will call you—a pretty, pretty gentleman! Ha!

JOR. And now, gentlemen, as our business is done, suppose we indulge in a little pleasure. Come and take a stroll round with me, gentlemen, and I'll show you the alterations that I'm going to make.

ALMA (*surprised*). Alterations, Mr. Jorgan?

JOR. Yes, Mrs. Suleny. You don't forget that I've got the remainder of your lease. I propose to take it up at Michaelmas, or sooner if quite convenient.

ALMA. But surely you cannot carry on the studios.

JOR. No. Nothing so useless.

ALMA. May I ask what you are going to do with it?

JOR. I'm going to establish our great Boot and Shoe and Closed Uppers Orphanage Asylum here. Yes, ladies and gentlemen, if you'll do me the honour to pay me a visit here six months from to-day, instead of a lot of lazy artists and Bacchantes philandering about the premises with next to nothing on,

I'll show you four hundred and fifty happy innocent little boot and shoe darlings, eating their bread and treacle, and drinking their milk and water, all of them well-washed, well-combed, and with manners and morals that are a credit to our profession. Good-day, Mrs. Suleny. Good-day, Sir Valentine. Come along, gentlemen, I'll show you the playground I've marked out for our little dears!

(*Exeunt* CORBY, SKEWETT, MODLIN, WAPES, L.)

SALLY. Oh, the little dears! I will see that playground!

(*Exit* JORGAN. SALLY *winks at him as he goes off and follows him.*)

BLAGG. Thomas, my son, you march straight home and walk up stairs, Thomas, to your room, and you take off your coat and trousers, Thomas, and you wait there till I come, Thomas, my son.

THOMAS (*in mortal fright*). Oh, crikey and Jeeroosalem!

(*Bolts off, followed by* BLAGG. POTE *approaches* SIR VALENTINE *meekly and humbly, on tiptoe.*)

SIR V. Well?

POTE. I'm the treasurer of our Boot and Shoe Orphanage.

SIR V. Indeed!

POTE. I trust you'll support us. (*Offers his hand.* SIR VALENTINE *very reluctantly gives his.*) I shall call on you for a subscription. (*Shakes hands very cordially, goes to door, and turns round with a sweet smile.*) I shall call on you for a subscription, Sir Valentine.

(*Exit* POTE, L. SIR VALENTINE, *speechless for a moment, shakes* POTE'S *grasp off his hand, stares helplessly at* ALMA. WILLIE *comes downstairs, and looks at the picture.* SIR VALENTINE *looks after* POTE *very savagely.*)

SIR V. If that man comes after me for a subscription——

LADY B. You'll give him one. How could you be so mad as to give money to that girl in front of all those people?

SIR V. Because I'd promised it to her.

LADY B. Then make such donations in private. Do you know what will be said of you?

SIR V. I don't know, and I don't care. But (*looking after* POTE) if that man calls on me for a subscription, I'll blow up his four hundred and fifty orphans, bread and treacle and all!

LADY B. (*shakes her head at him*). Come and see me to my carriage. (*To* ALMA.) You're to come back with me, my dear.

ALMA. Oh, but I've a lot of things to do. It will take me quite an hour.

LADY B. Then I'll send the carriage for you. At any rate, I'll try and save *your* reputation. (*Bows to* WILLIE.) Come, Val.

(*Exeunt* LADY BEAUBOYS *and* SIR VALENTINE, L.)

ALMA (*looking round*). A boot and shoe asylum! My poor father! Willie, did you hear?

WILLIE. Did you hear? My picture sold! Two hundred pounds! I can't bear to let her go.

ALMA (*very tenderly*). Willie, can't you cure yourself of this foolish fancy?

WILLIE. No — at least I shan't try.

ALMA. You must see that she is——

WILLIE. Speak it out!

ALMA. That she is utterly unworthy of you.

WILLIE. Yes, I see that, and I don't see that. I know it, and yet it's a lie. Look at her!

ALMA. How can you love a woman who is — not good?

WILLIE. What's that got to do with it? She can make me paint. Art's only hypocrisy, you know.

ALMA. Willie, that's not so!

WILLIE. Yes, I tell you. Art's hypocrisy. So's love! So's religion! When I was a child I was always pretending. Now I'm grown up I'm pretending still. If I were to say to myself, "This girl is, as I feel, as I know she is, light, wicked, heartless! She's all I daren't think of — she'd sell the immortal soul she has not got for a brooch or a bonnet," if I were once to say that of her, my hand would drop and I couldn't paint a stroke. So I say to myself, "She's divine, and I'm her mate! She's one half the universe and I'm the other! She's the dream of all the ages come true for one moment for me to paint!" When I stuff myself with such taradiddles — and believe them — it makes me worthy forty Titians, forty Raphaels! She's Helen, Cleopatra, Rosalind, Juliet, anything, and I'm her master! So I'll keep on loving her!

ALMA. I wish that she had never come, Willie.

WILLIE. When she goes, the world will be nothing but a boot and shoe asylum for orphans like me.

SALLY *enters* L. ALMA *goes to door,* R., *looks at* WILLIE *with great sympathy and interest. Exit* ALMA, R.

SALLY. Ah, my poor little fool! Some day

when I am ver' rich you shall paint me once more.

WILLIE. You'll be rich some day?

SALLY. Yes. A great milord is coming to fall in love with me. He will buy me dresses and pretty things just what I ask him. I shall say, "I love that villa." He will say, "It is nothing, I will buy it for you." "I love that ring." He will say, "It is yours." "I love those bracelets, those diamonds, those pearls," and he will chuck them all over me. I will be one great big plaster of diamonds all over here. (*Putting her hand over her chest.*) Ah! Ah! he is coming! I can see him (*putting up her two hands to her eyes, using them like spy-glasses and looking through them*), that great silly milord.

(WILLIE *looks at her, seizes her hands.*)

SALLY (*squeals*). Ah! Let me go! Let me go!

WILLIE. I hate you! I hate you!

(*Releases her; rushes to door*, R.)

SALLY. Ah, you are a fool!

WILLIE. Yes, I am. (*Rushes off*, R.)

SALLY (*goes to door*, R.; *beckons, calls off*). Pretty, pretty gentleman! (*Beckoning.*) Come here, pretty, pretty gentleman!

Enter JORGAN, L., *as if hypnotized, his whole manner and bearing as if he were doing it most unwillingly.*

SALLY. Pretty-pretty, you are rich, are you not? You like my picture?
JOR. (*boorishly*). No.
SALLY. That is one great big lie. You know you love me ver' ver' much. But you do not love me in this dress. Ah, you are right, you do not know how lovely I will be in a robe of blue velvet with beautiful gold lace.
JOR. No.
SALLY. Oh yes. Blue velvet — oh, I will be charming! And in red satin! What you think, beautiful red satin covered all over with shiny brights, like my eyes. Look at my eyes.
JOR. No. (*Same tone.*)
SALLY. Oh yes. And it will cost nothing but forty pounds.
JOR. Forty pounds! Don't you come any of your games on me! (*She winks at him.*) Forty pounds?
SALLY. Yes, I will tell you where to buy it. Ah, you are wicked!
JOR. No — no, I'm not.
SALLY. Yes, yes, you are as wicked as you

are beautiful. I can see it in your eye. (*Putting her finger nearly in his eye.*) Let me look in your eye. (*He submits, very troubled. She looks in his eye, suddenly squeals.*) Ah! (*Running away from him; he runs after her.*) Ah! Go away! You are wicked! Go away! Go away!

Enter POTE, L. JORGAN *stands solemn and stern.*

SALLY (*to* POTE). He is wicked that pretty, pretty gentleman. (*Exit*, R.)

POTE. Are you ready to go?

JOR. (*taking out purse*). In one moment, Pote; take this. (*Giving note.*)

POTE. What for?

JOR. Ten pounds for the new wing of the orphanage. Pote, there isn't a man in Market Pewbury that keeps a stricter watch on himself than I do, and if I'm ever led away for one moment from the strict path, I always make ample reparation. Take it. Order our pony round. I'll join you directly.

> (*Exit* POTE, L., *a little puzzled.* JORGAN *is following, at the door he suddenly turns, stands irresolute, goes up to door,* R., *where* SALLY *has gone off, checks himself, comes back to the picture, looks at it. His eye falls on*

the swords ranged round the room. He looks round carefully at all the doors, takes down a sword, stabs it through and through the picture, drops the sword, and creeps off noiselessly, R.)

CURTAIN.

(*Four months pass between Acts I. and II.*)

ACT II

SCENE THE SAME, THE PICTURE AND EASEL REMOVED

Discover WILLIE HESSELWOOD *in ulster and with travelling cap as if prepared for a journey.*

Enter ALMA, R.

ALMA. Ah, Willie, you're ready to start then?

WILLIE. Yes. London to-night! And straight away to Rome to-morrow morning, thanks to Sir Val. What a brick he has been to me!

ALMA. He has quite made up to you for the loss of the picture?

WILLIE. Yes, so far as money goes. But I'd give one of my ears and the tip of my nose to bring it home to that beast Jorgan.

ALMA. I'm afraid we shall never be able to prove it.

WILLIE. No. But I'm quite sure it was

Jorgan. However, it's no use crying over damaged Bacchantes!

ALMA. You've quite got over your foolish attachment to this girl?

WILLIE. Oh yes. That's all done with. Though just to make sure that I'm an interesting person, I pretend sometimes that I've got a cannon-ball here.

ALMA. Where?

WILLIE. Here, where my heart ought to be?

ALMA. I cannot understand ——

WILLIE. What?

ALMA. How you could have wasted your love on such a woman.

WILLIE. Oh, she fascinated me. I knew I was a fool, and I knew she was — what does it matter what she is? But I did love her! Yes, I did love her!

ALMA. Why haven't you done another picture of her?

WILLIE. I couldn't. The inspiration was gone. These last few months I've hated her.

ALMA. Why?

WILLIE. Oh, the moment I took off the property halo and the property wings I'd lent her, I saw she wasn't an angel at all, but only an animal.

ALMA. Why didn't you let me send her away?

WILLIE. Because I really wished to paint the picture for Sir Valentine.

ALMA. For Sir Valentine. (*Bitterly.*) Yes, I suppose her picture would have a great value for Sir Valentine.

WILLIE. No. It's not that. Sir Valentine only wished to have her picture for the sake of encouraging me.

ALMA. But you've heard — no, I won't speak of this gossip! But you might have told me, Willie. Then she would have gone, and we should have been spared all this scandal and disgrace.

WILLIE. I thought the old feeling for her would come back again. Now I know it never will. That's the reason I'm off to Rome. I shall get some fresh inspiration there.

ALMA. And do you take your property wings and property halo with you?

WILLIE. Yes, to stick them on the first thing in petticoats that meets me.

ALMA. Is that a man's love?

WILLIE. Well, it's an artist's.

ALMA. And the cannon-ball? Is that a property cannon-ball? And your heart, is it a property heart?

WILLIE. No, not altogether. I did love her, and she taught me how to paint, that's one comfort. I'll grind her down into pictures. I'll get some gorgeous flesh-tints out of her before I've done with her.

ALMA. Oh, Willie, you shan't say it's all hypocrisy. Art isn't hypocrisy.

WILLIE. No, not to the artist.

ALMA. Love isn't hypocrisy, religion isn't hypocrisy. Tell me before you go that love and religion are realities.

WILLIE. Yes, to everybody but the artist; but they must never be anything more than playthings to him, or he's done for.

Enter WHEELER, R., *announcing* LADY BEAUBOYS.

WILLIE. Good-bye. Thanks for all your goodness to me. Thanks again and again. (*Goes a step or two from her, returns.*) I want to tell you something before I go. Sir Val has only been good to me because he knew it would please you.

ALMA. Ah no! I can't believe that. Good-bye.

Enter LADY BEAUBOYS. *Exit* WHEELER.

ALMA. Mr. Hesselwood is leaving for Rome.

LADY B. Yes, so Sir Valentine told me. Good-bye, Mr. Hesselwood.

WILLIE. Good-bye, Lady Beauboys. I

shan't forget Sir Val's kindness, and I'll paint him a Bacchante some day! By Jove, my next Bacchante! She shall bewitch creation!
(*Exit*, L., *with great buoyancy.*)

ALMA. And now he is gone I can get rid of that girl. She must go to-day. (*Rings bell.*)

LADY B. My dear, of course she must go. I can't think why you've allowed the hussy to stay here so long.

ALMA. Willie said he couldn't paint his picture without her.

LADY B. He hasn't been able to paint it with her.

ALMA. What reason shall I give her for sending her away?

LADY B. Her conduct.

ALMA. What conduct?

LADY B. Surely to be seen in the High Street of Market Pewbury in a blue velvet dress with gold embroidery is sufficient reason of itself to prove that she is not a desirable inmate of any respectable house. To say nothing of the red satin with the spangles.

WHEELER *enters at door*, R.

ALMA. Will you find Mademoiselle Lebrune, and say that I wish to see her at once?
(*Exit* WHEELER, R.)

ALMA (*anxiously going to her*). Lady Beauboys, you fear — what I fear?

LADY B. I certainly should have thought that Val would have had better taste.

ALMA. Than to stoop to such a creature.

LADY B. Oh, I don't mean taste in creatures. I mean taste in dresses. The blue velvet! The red satin! Though certainly the hussy looks very piquante in them.

ALMA (*very anxiously*). Then, Lady Beauboys, you do think Sir Valentine——

LADY B. My dear, all this finery must come from some rich fool's pocket. There aren't many rich fools in Market Pewbury. If Val isn't the identical rich fool, who is? At any rate we'll give ourselves the benefit of the doubt, and start the baggage about her business.

ALMA (*bitterly*). How can men lower themselves?

LADY B. Ah, how can they, the wretches? How can they? How can they? How can they? The only answer to that conundrum is, "They can, and they do, and they will." As to Val, he's like every young man, that is, every healthy young man that ever lived. Nature has brought him to this great banquet of life and pleasure, given him an appetite, and spread the table in front of him. Do you think he'll turn his back on the feast because Market Pewbury shouts out that it's wicked to taste? No! He'll sit down to it. And its no use blaming him. If anybody is to blame, it's Nature.

ALMA. It seems to me that Nature is a dreadful bungler in everything that she does for women.

LADY B. Yes. There does seem to be a screw loose somewhere. But depend on it, after all, Nature is wiser than any of us, wiser than any old woman amongst us, wiser even than any *young* woman amongst us. And it's no good scolding her, for she will have her way. What we have to do as guardians of our homes, guardians of our children, guardians of what is called morality, is to behave ourselves, set a very high price on ourselves, make our homes attractive, and bash away the minxes. It's no use bashing away the men. That only drives them into the arms of the minxes. Now! We'll bash away this minx in blue velvet. Where is she?

ALMA. It's a hateful world. Are all men alike?

LADY B. Every son of the old Adam that I have ever met had a strong family likeness to his father.

ALMA. But Sir Valentine seemed so different——

LADY B. You mean that he has paid you a great deal of attention lately.

ALMA. I mean nothing. I was mistaken.

LADY B. No, my dear, I think not. I believe — I feel sure — that Val is really attached to you.

ALMA. Oh no, no! He can't be, or he wouldn't——

LADY B. My dear, trust me; I'm quite sure he cares for you, and when we've bashed away this minx——

ALMA (*indignantly*). What then? When the superior attractions of impudence, immodesty, and vulgarity are taken out of a man's way, then perhaps the feeble, wishy-washy charms of modesty, constancy, good manners, and ladyhood, may stand their poor little chance of captivating his heart! No, Lady Beauboys, I don't mind owning to you that I believe I could have cared very deeply for Sir Valentine, very, very deeply. But I won't (*almost in tears*) be second where this woman has been first, or (*dropping voice to bitter sneer*) fifty-first where she has been fiftieth.

LADY B. Very well, my dear. But don't deny yourself the satisfaction of seeing her safely off the premises.

Enter SALLY, R., *gorgeously arrayed in a blue velvet dress with gold trimmings, and a very large hat with broad ribbon strings, and smothered with bunches of flowers and feathers. She enters with great impudence and assurance, and cheerfully salutes them with a profound mock courtesy.*

SALLY (*blithely*). How do you do? (*To* ALMA, *who takes no notice.*) How do you do? (*To* LADY BEAUBOYS, *who glares very indignantly at her.*) I am ver' much glad to see you. (LADY BEAUBOYS *glares fiercely.*) You are not ver' much glad to see me? Well, I do not care one leetle, leetle d.

(LADY BEAUBOYS *indignantly points to her dress and hat.*)

SALLY (*looking at her dress*). What is the matter? You not like my dress? I think it goes me deuce well. (LADY BEAUBOYS *again points indignantly at the hat.*) Ah, my hat! (*Takes off her hat.*) He is tipsy, my hat! (*Smacks it, and then sticks it impudently on her head the wrong way. The roses and ribbons and feathers waggling.*) How you like that?

(*Wagging her head at* LADY BEAUBOYS.)

LADY B. (*sternly.*) Where did you get these clothes?

SALLY. At a shop in London. I go up

to London and I say to the patron, "Make me some pretty, pretty dresses. Make me so charming as will send every man cracked all over his head when he look at me!" He say, "Oh Mademoiselle, I cannot make you so charming as you are!" I say, "Get out! Be not a silly fool!" He say (*putting herself in a very languishing attitude, hand on breast*), "Oh, I cannot help myself when I look at you!" I say, "Get out! No D. N."

LADY B. (*solemnly*). What is "D. N."?

SALLY (*slowly and mysteriously*). "D. N." is what you say in England.

LADY B. (*trying to recollect, and turning to* ALMA *interrogatively*). We don't say "D. N." in England.

SALLY. No, you dare not say it, but you think it.

LADY B. What does it mean?

SALLY. Ask Sir Valentine; he will tell you. Well, I say to the patron, "Get out! No D. N. Make me the pretty, pretty dresses!" And he make them, and——

(*Strikes an attitude with outstretched arms, that shows off the dress.*)

LADY B. (*same stern, indignant tone*). Where did the money come from?

SALLY. From my pocket.

LADY B. From your pocket?

SALLY (*turns out the pocket of her dress; shows it quite empty*). See, I have made it quite empty.

LADY B. Yes; but you're making somebody else's pockets quite empty.

SALLY. Somebody else? Who is he?

LADY B. Yes. Who is he? Who is he? That's what I want to know. Who paid for this? (*Pointing to the dress indignantly.*) And this? (*Pointing to the hat.*) Do you hear? Who paid for them?

> (SALLY *strokes her chin, and then very slowly and elaborately winks at* LADY BEAUBOYS.)

LADY B. (*throws up her arms in despair; goes to* ALMA). My dear! Tell her to go!

ALMA (*who has been watching the scene with great interest*). Mademoiselle Lebrune, you will please to leave the studios this evening.

SALLY (*alarmed*). Leave the studios this evening! Where will I go?

ALMA. Where you please.

SALLY (*goes to* LADY BEAUBOYS). Where will I go? Where will I go?

LADY B. Go home to your mother, and ask her to take off all this flummery, and make a decent, respectable girl of you!

SALLY. No! I will not go home to my mother! I will not make a decent, respect-

ACT II THE TRIUMPH OF THE PHILISTINES 61

able girl of me! I will not leave the studios this evening.

ALMA. You will leave the studios this evening.

SALLY (*very firmly and defiantly bangs her hat on her head*). Ver' well! If I leave the studios I will make a great blow-up. Ha! Beware of this little bow-wow!
(*Showing her teeth.*)

LADY B. How dare you threaten us, you hussy!

SALLY. Hussy! I will not be a hussy! I will not be a female! Oh! You make me get out? Ver' well, somebody else who pay for this (*touching her dress*) and this (*touching her hat*) will get out with me. Ha! I will give Market Pewbury fits! And beans! And fireworks! I will flare up Market Pewbury! Hip! pip! Hooray! (*Claps her hat on her head.*) Hooray!

(*Exit* L. LADY BEAUBOYS *and* ALMA *stand looking at each other in dismay.*)

ALMA. What does she mean? Will she harm Sir Valentine? disgrace him?

Enter WHEELER, R., *announcing* SIR VALENTINE FELLOWES.

Enter SIR VALENTINE, R. *Exit* WHEELER.

SIR V. How d'ye do auntie? (*Approach-*

ing ALMA *very tenderly.*) How dy'e do, Mrs. Suleny?

ALMA (*coldly*). How do you do?

SIR V. I called to——(*stops embarrassed*). What's the matter?

ALMA. Will you please tell him, Lady Beauboys? (*Exit*, R.)

SIR V. (*looks after her*). Am I in disgrace?

LADY B. Don't you deserve it?

SIR V. Well, yes, generally. But what is the particular instance?

LADY B. This hussy.

SIR V. Which hussy?

LADY B. This one here. I think it is disgraceful of you men, when we shut our eyes as we do; when we make believe, as we do, that certain things have no existence; when the whole course of our social life is nothing more nor less than a huge organised deception for the purpose of masking your weakness and wickedness, and indulging our silly delusion that there is a single one of you that can be good and constant to us for a single hour'— I think it's disgraceful of you men not to play the game fairly and keep these impossible persons out of our way. They don't exist. There are no such people. Why won't you help us in keeping up the social sham when we do it all for your sake?

Sir V. That's a very pretty little sermon, auntie, but what's it got to do with me? I've played the game fairly. I've never pretended to be better nor worse than I am. I've never been ashamed of being a man, or wanted Nature to alter the whole course of her physiological economy to suit my convenience. And though I can't pretend to an unlimited stock of constancy, yet I think I've a passably good allowance — for a man. And as for any particular hussy — upon my word I don't know what you mean.

Lady B. This model creature — this Bacchante.

Sir V. I haven't seen her for some weeks. The last time I came here — well, auntie, I'll tell you the truth — I did have rather a narrow squeak — the little wretch set her cap at me — and I'd a jolly good mind — but Mrs. Suleny was here — I'm really fond of her — and — I was wise. Yes, it's the only time in my life that I've been when a pretty woman was concerned. But I was wise for once. I can say that for myself.

Lady B. Is that the truth, Val — the real downright truth?

Sir V. The real, downright truth, auntie.

That's the reason I've kept away from the studios. And I only came to-day to tell Mrs. Suleny that she won't be pressed again by the Market Pewbury tradesmen. Fentiman has been able to make an arrangement——

LADY B. With your money?

SIR V. Never mind how. She won't be troubled any more, and I'm trying to get back the lease of this place, so that she can carry on the studios.

LADY B. Well, I hope you won't succeed. High art will never flourish in Market Pewbury. No. Better wind it up and let Jorgan come in with his little bread-and-treacle darlings.

SIR V. And what will become of Mrs. Suleny?

LADY B. (*with meaning.*) Can't you find another career for her?

SIR V. I'll try.

(*The door bell is heard to ring off.*)

LADY B. It won't be a good match for you, Val, so far as money is concerned. But I like her, and it's my duty to get you married, and keep you out of mischief. (WHEELER *crosses from* R. *to* L. LADY BEAUBOYS *going to door*, R.; *comes back.*) Then it wasn't you who paid for the blue velvet dress?

SIR V. Not I.

LADY B. Nor the red satin?
SIR V. Not I.
LADY B. Then who did? (*Going off, very emphatically.*) Then who did.
  (*Exit,* R. WHEELER *admits* JORGAN *and* POTE, *door,* L. POTE *enters in his usual tiptoe way.* JORGAN *enters very apprehensively and nervously, a great change in his manner since the last Act.*)
JOR. (*to* WHEELER). Don't disturb Mrs. Suleny. Don't disturb anybody. Say that we merely wish to go upstairs and take a few measurements for the new dormitories if it is quite convenient.
  (*Looks round apprehensively. Exit* WHEELER, R. SIR VALENTINE *nods curtly at* JORGAN. JORGAN *nods curtly at* SIR VALENTINE. POTE *comes up to* SIR VALENTINE *in his offensively amiable way, holds out his hand, insists on shaking hands with* SIR VALENTINE.)
POTE. I hope I see you quite well, Sir Valentine.
SIR V. (*giving his hand reluctantly*). Thank you, Mr. Pote, I'm as well as can be expected under my present painful circumstances. (*Withdrawing his hand rather forcibly.*) I feel

F

a little better now. Mr. Jorgan, I sent Mr. Fentiman to you to propose that Mrs. Suleny should continue the lease of the studios. I'm prepared to pay you a very handsome price if you'll give her back the lease.

Jor. Quite impossible. I want to take over the premises at once, and as she's rather hard up, I should think it would answer her purpose to clear out and let us come in immediately. This is my great life-work, the establishment of this orphanage, and I want to hurry it on.

Sir V. But you can take your orphans elsewhere. There are other sites quite as desirable from the point of view of sanitation and morality, and quite as advantageous for the consumption of bread and treacle.

Jor. No there aren't. I'm going to make this spot a great centre of moral influence for the boot and shoe trade. I'm going to make a clean sweep of all the present abominations.

Sir V. Abominations, Mr. Jorgan! What abominations?

Jor. Artists, and pictures, and Bacchantes and so forth. Art itself is an abomination, and leads to all sorts of bad and evil courses.

Sir V. Are you speaking from experience, Mr. Jorgan?

Jor. Yes. At least not personal experience.

But I've seen quite enough of art to convince me it's not the sort of thing for Market Pewbury.

Sir V. Mrs. Suleny's father left her this place in trust. She thinks it's a sacred duty to obey him. If I offered you a very large sum ——

Jor. I shouldn't take it. I hold the lease of this place from your late uncle, and the very moment my term begins, out goes every manjack artist, every picture, everything and everybody in this place, out they go into the road at the very tick of the clock when I come in. Now, does that satisfy you?

Sir V. Quite. Good-day.

(*Is going off*, L.)

Pote (*follows him to the door, gets in his way*). I'm sorry we can't oblige you, Sir Valentine, but really I do think we're doing what is best for morality.

Sir V. Do you?

Pote. And, Sir Valentine (*stopping him*), I shall call on you for a subscription for our orphanage.

(*Offering his hand,* Sir Valentine *will not take it.*)

Sir V. Don't.

Pote (*very amiably*). Oh yes, I shall.

Sir V. Don't. I wish to treat every one

who comes to the Court with courtesy, but as sure as you come there for a subscription for any damned thing under the sun, I'll tell my servants to take you by the ear like this (*taking* POTE's *ear*), and kick you from the front door to the lodge gates.

(*Exit* L. POTE *stands aghast, terribly upset for some moments.*)

JOR. Now, Pote, let's make haste and get this job over. I don't want to hang about here.

POTE (*comes very slowly from the door, much ruffled in his meek way, turns round and looks after* SIR VALENTINE, *much upset*). Did you hear his language? And I've always been so nice to him.

(*Turns again and looks after* SIR VALENTINE *more in sorrow than in anger.*)

JOR. Never mind him. We shall get an opportunity of making a public example of him one of these days.

POTE (*still ruffled*). Yes. I always forgive my enemies, but I should like to make an example of him in the interests of morality.

JOR. Wait till he stands for Parliament. (*Looking round very nervously.*) I wish they'd come and let us see over those upstair rooms. We can't do with less than three more dormitories, can we?

POTE. We ought to have four, and then

we shall be overcrowding. You said something about another subscription ——.

Jor. Yes, but I can't afford it, Pote. My expenses have been very considerable lately.

Pote. You'll excuse me, but I do think you were a little too generous in giving that two hundred pounds to our widows' homes three months ago.

Jor. That was a peculiar gift, made under very peculiar circumstances.

Pote (*inquisitively*). What peculiar circumstances?

Jor. (*troubled*). Very peculiar circumstances, Pote. I cannot quite explain them.

Pote. You must have been tempted very much.

Jor. Tempted! Tempted! What leads you to suppose ——

Pote. Well, I know you make it a rule to keep a strict watch over yourself, and when you find yourself likely to be led astray, you sentence yourself to pay a fine to some charitable institution, don't you?

Jor. (*troubled*). Yes, yes. On some occasions I do — as a sort of moral compensation.

Pote. I do think it is such a splendid rule of conduct. How I do wish everybody would follow it! How all our charitable institutions throughout the land would benefit, wouldn't they?

Jor. Yes, yes, they would.

Pote (*very inquisitively*). I suppose on this occasion, eh? eh? — you must have been, eh? ——

Jor. Well, I don't mind owning to you, Pote, I was — I was placed in a most unfortunate position, Pote. Nine men out of ten would have forgotten themselves.

Pote. I *am* so glad you didn't forget yourself. And what was this unfortunate position?

Jor. We will not pursue the subject. Suffice it to say that I remembered what was due to myself and to Market Pewbury. I passed through the ordeal unscathed. What are you looking at?

Pote. Nothing! Nothing! So you resisted?

Jor. (*very indignantly*). Of course I resisted! (*Louder.*) Of course I resisted! Of course I resisted!

Pote. I *am* so glad. But what a large amount of moral compensation you would have paid if you had yielded, wouldn't you?

Jor. We'll drop the subject.

(Sally's *whistle heard off*, L.)

Pote (*who is standing opposite the door, looks off*). There's that Bacchante person. She's gone up to stroke our pony.

JOR. (*alarmed*). How dare she stroke our pony? How dare she stroke our pony?

SALLY (*outside*). Woa, woa, pretty, pretty! (*Whistling continued.*) Pretty, pretty, woa, woa, woa!

JOR. (*much frightened, bursts out*). Now, are we to be kept here all day? (*Stamping and shouting.*) My time's precious! I want to see over this building.

SALLY *enters* L., *whistling, stops on seeing* JORGAN.

SALLY. What is the matter, pretty, pretty gentleman?

JOR. (*taking no notice of her, goes to* POTE). Pote, go round the house to the other door, and ask them how they dare to keep me waiting like this!

(*Tries to get* POTE *off at door*, L.)

POTE (*a little protesting*). Yes, but what shall I say?

JOR. (*shouting him down, hustling him off at door*, L.). Go round and demand admission! I'm in my legal rights. I have the lease of this place. I want to make my plans for my new dormitories.

(*Bundles* POTE *off at door*, L., *turns to* SALLY, *stares at her in a helpless, pitiable way.*)

SALLY (*watching him comically*). Pretty, pretty gentleman, you are in a devil of a temper!

JOR. Yes, I am, so you'd better keep out of my way. Understand, madam, I decline to have anything to do with you. Our friendship, I mean our acquaintance, is at an end.
(*Very emphatically.*)

SALLY. Ah! See here, pretty, pretty gentleman. Do you see? (*Carefully opens one eye with her hand.*) Is there one leetle, leetle piece of green in that eye? No? Well, see in this other. (*Carefully opens the other for him to look in it.*) No?

JOR. I decline to look. I'm a respectable man, and I ask you in a respectable way, "Will you leave me alone, or will you compel me to take further proceedings?"

SALLY. I think I will compel you to take further proceedings. Yes, go on with your further proceedings.

(JORGAN *walks up aud down distressed and perplexed.*)

SALLY (*watches him and follows his motions with her finger*). Ah, that is ver' amusing when you show your pace! (*He stops.*) Woa, woa, pretty, pretty! Woa, woa! That is right. Woa, woa! (*He begins again, walking desperately, she still follows his motion with her finger.*) Gee up! Gee up! Pretty, pretty! (*Imitates*

ACT II THE TRIUMPH OF THE PHILISTINES

horse's action of walking.) Ah, I love you when you gee-up so beautiful like that!

JOR. (*comes to her desperately*). Once for all, I don't know you!

SALLY. Ah, that is what the funny, funny rascal thief say to the bobby-policeman. He say, "Get out, I not know you, Mr. Bobby!"

JOR. (*more firmly*). I don't know you. You are a thoroughly bad, disreputable person. And I wish you a very good day.

    (*Is stalking off towards door*, L. SALLY *darts in front of him, stops him, stands with her arms akimbo, her face bent forward to him.*)

SALLY (*defiantly*). Where you go, pretty-pretty?

JOR. (*firmly*). To inspect the buildings for my orphanage.

SALLY (*very determinedly, her face to him*). Go back, pretty-pretty. Go back, pretty-pretty! (*He steps backward a step or two, she follows him up.*) Go back!

    (*Driving him into the middle of the room.*)

JOR. (*backing*). Look here, don't you drive me to do something desperate——

SALLY (*squeals out at the top of her voice*). Ah, do what you thunder well please! Stand on your blessed mortal head! Fir' away! Hooray! Hooray! Hooray!

JOR. (*in an agony of fright*). Don't! Don't! Don't! Do be quiet, there's a good girl! (*Sinks into chair and cries.*) Oh, if I once get out of this mess! Oh, what a moral lesson it shall be to me! Oh, what a warning to the end of my days! (*Sobbing.*)

Enter POTE, L.

POTE (*inquisitively*). What's the matter?

JOR. (*with a ghastly attempt to be calm*). Nothing. Nothing. This person is suffering from a supposed insult.

SALLY. Get out! Nobody insult me! That is all D. N.

POTE. D. N.? What does she mean?

JOR. I don't know. I can't understand her. It's of no consequence. Are the rooms ready for our inspection?

POTE. The servant says they are being prepared, and we must wait here a few minutes till they're ready. But (*turning to* SALLY), dear me, dear me, what are you suffering from?

SALLY. I suffer from — no money. There is nothing else the matter with me. I have plenty of money — all right. I have not plenty of money, then you see I will bring what-you-call-him to Market Pewbury.

POTE. Bring who to Market Pewbury?

SALLY. The old Nick gentleman himself. Eh, pretty-pretty?

POTE. Pretty-pretty! What does she mean?

JOR. (*helplessly*). It's impossible to say. She keeps on calling me "pretty-pretty"— a most inappropriate familiarity. I can't understand it. We'll go and inspect the washhouses, shall we?

(*Taking* POTE'S *arm, leading him off.*)

SALLY. I will go and inspect those washhouses.

JOR. Not now, my good creature.

(*Trying to get* POTE *off.*)

SALLY. Yes, my good creature. I will inspect, and when the little duckies come I will be their mother, and give them their breads and treacles.

JOR. (*fiercely*). You can't! You can't! Come along, Pote.

SALLY (*very determinedly. Same action as before*). Go back, pretty-pretty! Go back!

JOR. Perhaps I'd better listen to what she has to say, Pote. You go round to the other door.

POTE. But I've been, and they told me to wait here.

JOR. (*frenzied, shouts*). I will not wait! I insist! I will not be kept waiting! Go and tell them, Pote, that I insist on my legal rights, as the owner of this house, to inspect the upstairs premises at once. Go!

(*Exit* POTE, L.)

JOR. You won't be satisfied till you've ruined me, I suppose. Why won't you take yourself off, like a dear, good girl?

SALLY. Take myself off? Where will I go with myself?

JOR. Go back to the Continent.

SALLY. Ver' well, give me plenty money, and I take myself off?

JOR. I can't give you any more money. I've overdrawn at the bank, and I'm in a terrible mess. Mr. Pote begins to suspect me— Mrs. Jorgan begins to suspect me. They're both watching me.

(*Groans, looks at her helplessly.*)

SALLY. Mr. Respectable man, you are pickled!

JOR. Look here! I've come to the end of my tether.

SALLY. Tether? That is money?

JOR. Yes, in this case. Not another sixpence.

SALLY. Ver' well, sir. Then *I* must take further proceedings, sir.

JOR. Further proceedings?

SALLY (*nods*). Mrs. Suleny say to me, "Get out!" I say to you, "Mr. Respectable man, you get out with me." Then the band will play.

Jor. Band! What for?

Sally. To march us out of Market Pewbury, you and me, Mr. Respectable man, and everybody will look at us.

Jor. You don't mean to say you're going to expose me before Market Pewbury?

Sally. Yes, I will expose you, if you will not expose me plenty of money.

Jor. Don't I tell you it's impossible — simply impossible. (*Groans.*) Oh, what a punishment this is! Surely I don't deserve such a punishment as this! Oh, what a moral lesson it shall be to me! (*Sits and sobs.*)

Enter Sir Valentine, L.

Sir V. I beg pardon! I thought I should find Mrs. Suleny here.
(*Looks from one to the other a little puzzled, withdraws,* L.)

Jor. (*lifts his face, which shows a sudden illumination. He rises very slowly, follows* Sir Valentine *to the door, looks after him, comes stealthily up to* Sally, *pauses, looks at her, then, with an intensely sinister suggestion, whispers*). Would you like to be my lady?

Sally (*looks at him inquiringly*). Get out!

Jor. I mean it. Now listen to this. Don't you be a fool. It's no good your hanging on to me. I won't give you another penny. Do you understand that? Not another penny! If you expose me you'll ruin me, but you'll ruin yourself as well. You do as I tell you, and you can be my lady.

SALLY. My lady? What my lady?

JOR. My Lady Fellowes, and live at the Court. How would you like that?

SALLY. Oh, that suit me perfectly to the ground. But there is no leetle bit of green in Sir Valentine's eyes.

JOR. No, but there is a very strong public feeling in Market Pewbury.

SALLY. Public feeling? What is that?

JOR. Public feeling always runs very high in England on questions of morality.

SALLY. Morality? What is morality?

JOR. Morality compels people to conduct themselves properly for fear of being found out.

SALLY. Oh, you have plenty much morality here in England. But me — I have not ver' much morality myself, and how will I be my Lady Fellowes?

JOR. It is already suspected in Market Pewbury that Sir Valentine bought you these dresses.

SALLY (*looks at him*). Oh, Mr. Respectable man!

JOR. When it's known that he has compromised you, a wave of public indignation will sweep over the community, and he'll be obliged to marry you.

SALLY. Marry me? Get out? He will not be such a fool!

JOR. (*staring round*). Hush! He can't help himself. You don't know what English feeling is in these matters. I tell you he'll be obliged to marry you, or make you a handsome provision.

SALLY. I have no want of provisions. I have want of plenty money.

JOR. And he'll be obliged to give it to you.

SALLY. What for why?

JOR. Because he has compromised you.

SALLY. Ah, get out? You make larks of me!

JOR. No, no! You stick to it that Sir Valentine is the guilty party, and I'll take care that public opinion will make him behave honourably to you.

SALLY. Behave honourably? Is that I will be my Lady Fellowes? (JORGAN *nods*. SALLY, *clapping hands*.) Oh, that is what I was borned for! I will love to be that. I will have plenty of dresses and carriages! (*Clapping her hands*.) You are sure about that public feeling?

JOR. Quite sure. Leave that to me.

SALLY. Ah, you are ver' funny peoples in England!

JOR. (*suggestively*). Then it was Sir Valentine who bought you these dresses! (SALLY *winks.*) You might perhaps wink at him.

SALLY. Winks not catch him. He not such a silly fool as you was. I will find another little bit of salt for him.

JOR. (*looking off*, L.). He's coming.

SIR VALENTINE *enters.* JORGAN *utters a deep "Oh!" of relief, and exit.* SIR VALENTINE *has entered very carelessly, whistling; is crossing from* L. *to* R. *without taking any notice of Sally.*

SALLY (*calls*). My Valentine!
SIR V. (*stops halfway across*). Well?
SALLY. Where you go?
SIR V. To find my aunt and Mrs. Suleny.
                    (*Going a step or two*, R.)
SALLY (*again stopping him*). My Valentine!
SIR V. Well?
SALLY. Why you run away from me? I am so ugly, eh?
SIR V. You are perfectly charming.
                    (*At door.*)
SALLY (*makes him a very polite, impudent bow.*) Oh, sir, I think you have the ver' best taste of any gentleman I ever meet!
SIR V. (*returns the bow with great mock cour-*

tesy). Mademoiselle, you have such exquisite taste yourself (*glancing at her dress*), that I accept your compliment as the severest truth.
(*Going to door.*)

SALLY. My Valentine! (SIR VALENTINE *turns; she beckons him.*) Will you please to come here for one little second?

SIR V. (*stands irresolutely at the door a minute or two*). No. (*Opens door; turns and looks at her.* SALLY *beckons again.* SIR VALENTINE *stands irresolutely for a moment, then shuts door; comes up to her.*) What the devil mischief now?

SALLY. If I am so charming, why you not try to catch me?

SIR V. Because I should succeed.

SALLY. You not wish to succeed? Why not?

SIR V. Because I cannot consider you as a type of the young man's best companion.

SALLY. Oh yes, I make the jolly best companion for every young man.

SIR V. Alas! I fear I cannot accept you as a desirable acquaintance.

SALLY. What is desirable?

SIR V. Desirable in one sense implies an absence of those qualities that make you so perfectly desirable in another!

SALLY. What qualities make me desirable acquaintance?

SIR V. Well, a little dash of modesty——

G

SALLY. Ver' well. How much?

SIR V. Ah, that's the point!

SALLY. I will have just as much modesty as you thunder well please.

SIR V. I'm sure you will. I'm sure all you ladies will have, or pretend to have, just that amount of modesty that you think will make you attractive to us. But I'm speaking of the other sort of modesty.

SALLY. Ah, the other sort?

SIR V. Natural modesty. Modesty *au naturel.*

SALLY. Modesty *au naturel.* What is that?

SIR V. I'm afraid you wouldn't understand it.

SALLY. No matters about modesty *au naturel.* I do ver' well without that, eh?

SIR V. (*looking at her half contemptuous, half attracted*). Upon my word, yes. The least suspicion of modesty would spoil you entirely. You're perfect beyond perfection as you are!

SALLY (*making him another mock bow*). Oh, sir, when you speak all the mortal truth like that, you make me blush right straight to those tips of my blessed toes. (*Putting her toe out beneath her dress.*)

SIR V. (*moves a step or two towards her*). Ah!

SALLY. Shall I tell you a secret? When I was to London the old woman tell me my fortune.

SIR V. And what was your fortune my pretty — maid?

SALLY. She say a "fine young English gentleman is coming to love you with all his heart."

SIR V. Fair or dark?

SALLY. I will show him to you. Come here! (*She goes up stage.*) Do you hear? Come here when I tell you! Take that chair! Put it here! (*Making him put chair in front of fireplace and looking-glass.*) Now that other one. Put it there! (*Jumps up on one.*) Now be up in that chair! (*He hesitates. She speaks very commandingly, rapping on the mantleshelf with her knuckles.*) Do you hear? Be up in that chair and do what the devils I tell you. (*He jumps up beside her. She turns his head towards the looking-glass, points.*) There is that beautiful young Englishman who is going to love me with all his heart.

SIR V. (*throwing off restraint*). The devil he is! (*Puts his arm round her waist.*)

ALMA *enters in gallery*, R.

SALLY (*continuing*). The old woman say, "You will make a lovely, lovely picture together, you two!"

SIR V. (*looking in the glass*). Upon my word we do, don't we?
(ALMA *has come downstairs.* SIR VALENTINE *sees her in the looking-glass. He turns his face right round to* ALMA, *shows great shame.*)

SIR V. Mrs. Suleny!
(*Gets off chair, stands showing intense shame.*)

ALMA (*coming downstairs*). I fear I've intruded! Pray consider my house at your service. But perhaps it's unnecessary to tell you that. (*Going off*, R.)

SIR V. (*crossing towards her*). Mrs. Suleny, let me explain——

ALMA. Surely there's no need. Everything is perfectly intelligible.

SIR V. But you do not believe——

ALMA. My own eyesight? I'm afraid I must. (*Going off.*)

SIR V. (*again stops her*). Mrs. Suleny, this young lady will explain that—that she has not the slighest claim upon me in the world. (*To* SALLY.) Is it not so? (*To* ALMA.) Ask her yourself.

ALMA (*comes from door to* SALLY, *who has got off chair and come down stage*). Who gave you that dress?
(SALLY *steals a look at* SIR VALENTINE, *says nothing.*)

SIR V. Do you hear? Why don't you speak?

SALLY. Sir Valentine gives me the money (SIR VALENTINE *starts*) and I buy it in London.

SIR V. I gave you the money?

SALLY. Here in this blessed room.

ALMA. You hear?

(*A slight shrug of the shoulders, turns.*)

SIR V. Mrs. Suleny! On my honour——

ALMA. Ah! not that stale word, if you please.   (*Exit,* R.)

SIR V. (*turns round on* SALLY). I gave you money? I gave you nothing but that one ten pounds.

SALLY. Ah, but I spend it so well, I buy all these dresses with it.

SIR V. What?

SALLY. That is so on my honour.

SIR V. (*goes to bell, rings it*). You'll explain to Mrs. Suleny that you have no claim on me—that this is a mistake.

SALLY. Ah! there is no mistake.

Enter WHEELER, R.

SIR V. Will you ask Mrs. Suleny if she will be kind enough to step here for one moment?   (*Exit* WHEELER.)

Sir V. You will tell Mrs. Suleny the truth?

Sally. Oh yes, all the blessed mortal truth. That you love me ver' much——

Sir V. What?

Sally. And you will have honourable intentions.

Sir V. I have the most honourable intentions to keep out of your way for the future!

Sally. Ah! you think that you will keep out of my way! Oh no! You will keep ver' much in my way.

Re-enter Wheeler.

Wheeler. Mrs. Suleny is engaged, Sir Valentine, and cannot see you.

Sir V. I must see her. Please to say that it is most important. I must see her.

(*Exit* Wheeler, R.)

Sir V. Now, let me understand you. What the devil do you mean?

Sally. Oh, sir, you know ver' well! You are the guilty party.

Sir V. Guilty party! Guilty of what?

Sally. You have compromised me. You love me ver' much. I love you ver' much. And now we come to business.

Sir V. Business?

SALLY. Public feeling runs very high in England.

SIR V. Public feeling?

SALLY. On questions of morality.

SIR V. Morality? What have you and morality got to do with each other? (*Takes her by the hand, drags her towards* R.) You'll come with me to Mrs. Suleny——

Enter WHEELER, R.

WHEELER. Mrs. Suleny is not at home, Sir Valentine.

(*Exit* WHEELER. SIR VALENTINE *drops her arm, stands perplexed.*)

SALLY. Ah! (*Coming up to him.*) You see you must behave honourably to me. You must make me your lady!

SIR V. (*seizes both her arms*). Make you my lady! I'll see you at the devil first!

(*Throws her into the rocking-chair. She rocks to and fro singing a snatch of a French song. He walks up and down the room in a tempest of indignation, shame, anger, and bewilderment.*)

CURTAIN.

(*Two days pass between Acts II. and III.*)

ACT III

Scene — the same

Afternoon. Discover JORGAN, WAPES, MODLIN, CORBY, BLAGG, *and* SKEWETT. *They have just been shown in by* WHEELER, *who is crossing to* R.

WHEELER. If you'll wait here a few minutes, gentlemen, I'll see if the studios are ready for you.

JOR. (*who is evidently in very good spirits*). No hurry! no hurry! Tell Mrs. Suleny to suit her own convenience. She's leaving to-day?

WHEELER. Yes, sir, this evening. She expected to leave this morning, but found she wasn't quite ready.

JOR. (*genially*). No hurry! no hurry! We're so overcrowded in our present place that I've been obliged to bring on my first batch of orphans to-day. But no hurry, so long as we can give the poor little dears a shakedown for the night. (WHEELER *is going off*, R.)

JOR. (*calls him*). Ha!—have all the other inmates cleared out?

WHEELER. Everybody except Mademoiselle Lebrune.

JOR. Mademoiselle Lebrune? You allude to the young French female?

WHEELER. Yes, sir.

JOR. And why is she allowed to stay?

WHEELER. Well, sir, we can't get rid of her. Mrs. Suleny have told her to be off; but, so far as I can gather from her language, she says that she'll see Mrs. Suleny — hem — further first. She means to stick here till Sir Valentine comes for her, she says. And an hour ago, sir, she sends off a telegram to Sir Valentine asking him to send a carriage and pair to take her to the Court. It's the rummest go as ever I heard on.

(*Giving way to an involuntary laugh.*)

JOR. (*sternly*). Don't laugh! It's no laughing matter.

WHEELER. No, sir.

JOR. Tell Mrs. Suleny that the town council have come to take formal possession.

WHEELER. Yes, sir.   (*Exit*, R.)

WAPES. This is a shocking business to have happening right under our very noses.

BLAGG. Likewise the noses of our wives! Likewise our daughters! Likewise our sons!

SKEW. Drive 'em out of the town, I say!

Brand 'em and drive 'em forth from out our midst!

JOR. Yes. Let this be a great moral lesson to us all! Let it be a warning of the awful mire a man gets sunk into when he once leaves the straight path of moral duty and respectability. And let us all be thankful that we are, I trust, completely fortified.

MOD. (*looking up to the ceiling*). Well, I can speak for myself.

WAPES. Yes, it'd take a good deal in the way of feminine corruptibility to lead me astray.

CORBY. So it would me. When I was in London last bank holiday, a very pretty woman, in a blue dress, comes up to me quite in a larky way——

JOR. (*sternly*). We are not assembled to discuss females in blue dresses. We are here to install our first batch of orphans. (*Uneasily.*) I can't think what has become of Pote——

WAPES. I met him at the station yesterday morning. He said he was going to London on very particular business. Ain't he come back?

JOR. No; and he knows we take possession to-day. Now, gentlemen (*looks all round, rubs his hands genially*), whilst we're waiting, as you're all subscribers to the asylum, I think we might decide what we'll do here. This is to be the dining-room; and I think, to start with, we'll make a clean sweep of all this.

(*Pointing to the hangings and decorations.*)

SKEW. Burn it, burn it! Don't let it lead the minds of the orphans from higher things. Burn it!

JOR. You're an upholsterer, Mr. Wapes, and, with the sanction of my committee, I shall propose that you cart away all this rubbish, and re-decorate this hall in a chaste and suitable way.

WAPES. Yes, I've got some nice new patterns in curtains and wall-papers, just fresh down from Tottenham Court Road, very pretty and artistic.

SKEW. Artistic! We won't have anything artistic here. I shall withdraw my subscription.

WAPES. Don't fly out, Mr. Skewett! There's different ways of being artistic. Some people are artistic in one way, and some people are artistic in another. Let everybody be artistic in his own way. That's my motto as an upholsterer.

SKEW. (*viciously blinking all round*). Burn it, I say! burn it all!

WAPES. Quite so. Burn all this, if you like (*sweeping his hand round*); because it's in bad taste. Looking at it as an upholsterer, I call it in very bad taste. But don't burn things that are artistic according to the taste of Market Pewbury!

JOR. Well, at any rate, we'll do away with all this. (*Sweeping his hand round; bell rings off*, L.) And we'll make a fresh start. I can't tell you, gentlemen, how I shall devote myself to the work of purifying the moral atmosphere of this place, and making it a beacon light to the great staple industry of Market Pewbury.

(WHEELER *crosses from* R. *to* L., *and goes to door.*)

JOR. (*proceeding cordially*). Let's get to business, gentlemen! Don't let the grass grow under our feet. Remember, our first band of little pilgrim orphans are already on their peaceful war-path. I dare say they are now carolling in the train, and making every station along the line resound with their joyous melody.

WHEELER (*comes from door*, L., *and brings telegram to* MR. JORGAN). Sent on from your manufactory, sir. (*Exit*, R.)

JOR. (*taking it*). I daresay this is from Pote.

(*Opens it; looks uneasy and puzzled.*)

WAPES. Is it from Mr. Pote?

JOR. Yes.

WAPES. And what does he say?

JOR. I don't understand it. "Don't proceed further with Orphanage till you have seen me. Most important. Shall reach Pewbury two forty-five." (*Taking out watch.*) He'll be here directly.

Enter ALMA, L. JORGAN *continues to look at telegram very anxiously.*

ALMA. The west wing is now quite cleared, Mr. Jorgan, if you wish to take possession.

JOR. Thank you, Mrs. Suleny. I'm much obliged to you for clearing out before your time.

ALMA. Don't mention it. I wished to leave Market Pewbury, and it answers my purpose to let you come in at once.

Enter WHEELER, R., *announcing* LADY BEAUBOYS. *Enter* LADY BEAUBOYS *with a light shawl, parasol, and fan; during the following scene she takes off the shawl, and puts all three of them on chair. Goes to* ALMA, *shakes hands.*

ALMA. Wheeler, show these gentlemen to the west wing, and give them the keys.

WHEELER. This way, gentlemen.

(*Exit*, R. *Exeunt* CORBY, BLAGG, MODLIN, WAPES, SKEWETT, *and* JORGAN. JORGAN *goes last, reading over the telegram very anxiously.*)

LADY B. My dear! (*Kisses* ALMA.) Has Sir Valentine arrived?

ALMA. Arrived? No. At least, I've not heard. He wrote to me yesterday.

LADY B. And you didn't reply! Naughty girl! Now about this hussy! Where is she?

ALMA. I've told her to go.

LADY B. Why haven't you turned her out?

ALMA. Because — because I'm still weak and foolish enough to let her stay here rather than she should cause disgrace to Sir Valentine.

LADY B. What further disgrace can she cause him? The story's all over the country. Some correspondent has sent an account to the London papers, and they're full of it. She can surely do him no further harm.

ALMA. I don't know. I believe I'm foolish enough to let her stay here because — oh, isn't it weak of me?— I've been afraid that she'll go to him! (*Ring at door*, L.)

LADY B. My dear, he's coming here, and if you don't see him ——

ALMA. What then?

LADY B. The wretch has actually telegraphed to him to bring a carriage and pair to fetch her.

(WHEELER *crosses from* R. *to* L.; *goes to door.*)

ALMA. Well?

LADY B. As soon as he received the telegram he ordered the new landau and his pair of chestnuts, and he's driving up here for that hussy.

ALMA. What?

LADY B. My dear, if you don't take him in hand, I do believe he'll drive with that baggage and all her baggage through Market Pewbury in an open landau!

ALMA. No! No! Impossible!

(WHEELER *comes from door*, L.)

WHEELER. Sir Valentine Fellowes is outside, ma'am.

ALMA. I'm not at home.

SIR VALENTINE *enters*, L.

ALMA (*very coldly, with great dignity*). I'm not at home. (*Exit*, R., *followed by* WHEELER. SIR VALENTINE *stands nonplussed.*)

LADY B. (*vigorously*). Well, now I hope you're thoroughly well satisfied with yourself.

SIR V. (*grimly*). If I'm not I ought to be. Look at that.

(*Giving her a newspaper to read.*)

LADY B. (*hastily scans it*). You've brought it all on yourself, Val. You may as well try to batter down a mountain with your fists as try to demolish that dull hard mixture of stubborn virtue and stupid hypocrisy which go to make up English middle-class respectability. Give it up, Val! See where you are! And all through what?

Sir V. All through not being an out-and-out hypocrite like the rest of my neighbors.

Lady B. A little decent hypocrisy is the first chemisette that human nature puts on when it grows out of fig leaves. See what you've lost through not wearing that chemisette!

Sir V. I don't mind a chemisette. But I do object to being cuffed, and muffled, and bandaged, and buckled up into compulsory decency.

Lady B. When you're at sea you must obey the rules of the road at sea. When you're on land you must obey the rules of the road on land. If you go to the right when it's the rule of the road to go left, you only get smashed up. Now there's no living in England without going to the right when people are looking. You can go to the left as much as you like when their eyes are turned the other way.

Sir V. But I haven't gone to the left!

Lady B. What!

Sir V. That's the devil of it! That's the hardship of my position! I don't mind being the hero of a scandal, but let me do something to deserve it! Let me break some woman's heart, ruin her reputation, carry her off from some other lover, shoot her husband, drive her to drown herself! As it is, I'm a wretched sham! I've won the Victoria Cross of devilry and gallantry, and I've done nothing! Not even kissed a chambermaid — at least, not lately!

LADY B. You were making love to this French hussy two days ago.

SIR V. Not seriously. And I was interrupted even at that!

LADY B. Your arm was round her waist.

SIR V. Yes, it was. And that's my sole reward, my only compensation, for having lost the woman whom I do really love; for having forfeited the respect of all my neighbors; for being pointed at in the public streets; and being chaffed and bullied in all the newspapers. And for being left with the prospect of having to pay this French beauty a lot of money to get rid of her, or have her hanging round my neck for the rest of my life!

LADY B. Your own fault for not obeying the rule of the road at Market Pewbury.

SIR V. Damn Market Pewbury!

LADY B. It's no use damning Market Pewbury. It's a good average bundle of humanity, I assure you. Remember, Val, the world only goes on and hangs together because of the virtue and respectability in it. Hypocrisy and humbug don't hold a community together.

Neither does immorality, however charming and delightful it may be. And though there's a good deal of cant and humbug in Market Pewbury, there's a good deal of sturdy virtue and honesty too.

SIR V. Ah, just a trifle too much, don't you think?

LADY B. My dear boy, a certain average of human conduct has got to be maintained somewhere in the world. And I think we sinners ought to be very grateful to the good people who commit these excesses in virtue and respectability, as it gives us a chance of striking the balance on the other and pleasanter side without any danger to the general morals of the community. Come now! What do you mean to do?

SIR V. I mean to strike a good balance on the other and pleasanter side.

LADY B. How?

SIR V. I've lost my character. That's all right. I've spent a great deal of money in paying her father's debts and trying to make her happy. That's all right. I've lost her and she thinks me a deceiver and a libertine. That's all right. I'm stared at and pointed at in Market Pewbury, and blackguarded all over the country. That's all right. That's my credit account. I've paid my scot to English respectability without grumbling. Now I'm going to have some fun for my money!

LADY B. What are you going to do?

SIR V. I'm going to paint myself ten times blacker than Market Pewbury thinks me. My income is fifteen thousand a year. I'm going to spend it all for three years in raising the deuce and shocking Market Pewbury!

SALLY *enters*, R., *in flame-coloured red satin dress, covered with spangles, and hat to match.*

LADY B. My dear Val——

SIR V. My dear auntie——

(LADY BEAUBOYS *catches sight of* SALLY, *draws herself up with great hauteur.*)

SALLY (*kisses her hand to* LADY BEAUBOYS). Ah! My dear auntie, I hope I see you ver' jolly fit to-day!

LADY B. You unspeakable creature, how dare you address yourself to me!

(*Turns her back on* SALLY.)

SALLY (*puts up both of her hands to her nose at* LADY BEAUBOYS' *back, and winks at* SIR VALENTINE). Ah, my Valentine! You got my telegram?

SIR V. Yes, mademoiselle.

SALLY. And you bring your carriage and gee-gees to elope away with me?

SIR V. They are outside, mademoiselle.

SALLY. And I will have your two footmens, with all that flour on their heads (*gesture*), to march after me when I walk myself about?

SIR V. They are at your service, mademoiselle.

SALLY. Listen to this, Auntie Beauboys!

> (LADY BEAUBOYS *looks at her with unutterable disdain, sweeps by her, rings the bell.* SALLY *makes a grimace at her, calls* SIR VALENTINE'S *attention by a gesture of the thumb.*)

SALLY. And when we be married, my Valentine?

SIR V. Never.

SALLY. Never? You not marry me, my Valentine?

SIR V. Not if you were the only charmer of your adorable sex on this unenchanted island.

SALLY. Ah, well — see here, my Valentine — if you not marry me, I will make that public feeling in England run up ver' high (*gesture*) — right up to the blessed ceiling, on questions of morality.

SIR V. Exactly. Make public feeling run as high as you please. That's just what I want you to do.

SALLY. What you say?

Enter WHEELER, R.

LADY B. Please to find my footmen, and bring them here to me.

(*Exit* WHEELER, L.)

SIR V. (*to* SALLY). Make public feeling run up sky-high! I'll help you, and pay you very handsomely.

SALLY. What? You pay me? Ver' well. What will I do?

SIR V. I want you to spend the next three years of your life in shocking Market Pewbury in any and every possible way that your lively imagination can devise.

SALLY. Shock Market Pewbury! Ver' well. Listen to this, Auntie Beauboys!

SIR V. That dress of yours is altogether too modest and quiet——

SALLY. Ah! (*Looking down it.*) What you think, Auntie Beauboys?

SIR V. Get something a little gayer and smarter.

SALLY. Ver' well. You pay?

SIR V. Certainly. Something really startling.

SALLY. All right. What colour you think suit me best, Auntie Beauboys?

SIR V. You'll find it rather dull work shocking Market Pewbury all alone. I'll provide you with a whole regiment of congenial associates.

SALLY (*with a wild shriek of delight*). Regiment! Soldiers! Listen to *that*, Auntie Beauboys!

SIR V. No, not soldiers. But you have doubtless a good sprinkling of friends with your own tastes and habits — your own particular chums, eh?

SALLY. Oh yes, I have good sprinkling of ver' particular chums.

SIR V. Invite them all down to Market Pewbury. Get rooms for them at the Bull and George, and all the best hotels. Ask them to thoroughly enjoy themselves at my expense, and make things hum all over the town.

SALLY. Oh yes, we will make things hum at the Bull and George, and all over the town. What more, my Valentine?

SIR V. Do just whatever you please. We'll have a three years' carnival in Market Pewbury! We'll paint the town one universal blazing red!

Re-enter, L., WHEELER, *with two* FOOTMEN.

LADY B. (*to* WHEELER). Go to your mistress and ask her to please send me a maid to pack this person's belongings.

WHEELER. Yes, my lady. (*Exit*, R.)

LADY B. (*to the* FOOTMEN). Come with me and bring this person's boxes down, and put them on the carriage.

SALLY. What you do with my boxes?

LADY B. You unmentionable hussy, I'm going to take your boxes and your clothes and every rag you have, except what you stand upright in, and I won't go to my bed this night till I've seen you and them safely out of this town, you unutterable creature!

SALLY (*shouts*). Hi! Some bobbies here! She steal my luggages! Hi! Some bobbies, some policemens here!

Enter ALMA, R., *followed by* WHEELER.

ALMA. What's the matter?

SALLY. Auntie Beauboys goes to steal all my luggages. (*Runs to* SIR VALENTINE.) What will I do? Tell me what I will do now?

SIR V. Go and look after your boxes.

SALLY. Ah! (*Bolts off*, R.)

LADY B. My dear, have I your permission to turn that person and her belongings out of your house?

ALMA. The house is Mr. Jorgan's now.

LADY B. Then I'll turn her out of Mr. Jorgan's house, and I'm sure he ought to be very much obliged to me. (*To* WHEELER.) Send the maids to me, and take me to that person's room.

WHEELER. This way, my lady. (*Exit*, R.)

LADY B. (*to the* FOOTMEN). Follow him, and do as I tell you.

(*Exeunt* FOOTMEN, R. ALMA *is going.* LADY BEAUBOYS *stops her.*)

LADY B. (*aside to her*). Do take pity on him! He'll go to the dogs if you don't. Remember what we women are sent into this world for — remember there is no reason for our existence except to save these poor wretches of men from following their natural bent of going to the dogs. Do save him!

ALMA (*going off, protesting*). Lady Beauboys——

LADY B. My dear, I'll see to this lady. (*At the door.*) We'll have no carnival at Market Pewbury, and the town shall not be painted red. (*Exit*, R.)

SIR V. Mrs. Suleny, I wrote to you yesterday asking your pardon. You did not answer.

ALMA (*a little coldly*). There was no answer.

SIR V. You'll forgive me?

ALMA. I've forgotten it.

SIR V. (*very tenderly*). You'll forgive me!

ALMA. I say, I have forgotten it. There's no more to say.

Sir V. At least you will let me explain.

Alma. There can be nothing to explain. Surely it's intelligible enough. You thought you were abroad ——

Sir V. I was abroad. I was away from my best self.

Alma. Indeed; and is that a frequent occurrence with you?

Sir V. Not since I've known you.

Alma. Surely I can have made no difference to your — to your escapades from your best self.

Sir V. Don't I tell you since I've known you ——

Alma. They have been less frequent. That is very flattering to me. I sincerely hope they will be less frequent still in the future. Good day. (*Going.*)

Sir V. (*intercepts her*). No; you shan't go till you understand ——

Alma. Very well, let me understand. Let me understand how it is, after your words to me only a few days ago — ah, you don't know how I treasured them! — how it is that the moment I'm away from you, you can forget me, forget yourself, make yourself cheap to the cheapest creature within your reach. Let me understand how it is that men do these things?

Sir V. Because we are men, and because there is no folly or madness too great for us where a woman is concerned.

Alma. And have you much folly and madness to answer for? (*Pause.*) Why don't you speak?

Sir V. Surely you don't wish me to speak of what must give you pain?

Alma. But I do, I do, I do. I won't forgive you unless you tell me all your past follies and madnesses.

Sir V. (*changing to a light, chaffing tone*). Very well, then I'll make short work of them. I've been the very, very worst rascal that ever lived, and there's an end of it.

Alma. I don't believe you.

Sir V. But I have. But bad as I've been in the past, it's nothing to what I shall be in the future if you don't forgive me.

Alma. I don't believe you. You haven't been so — so — so thoroughly bad?

Sir V. (*same light, chaffing tone*). No; on the contrary, I have been remarkably good. In fact, if any man in this world has been thoroughly and entirely blameless, that man is myself.

Alma. I don't believe you.

Sir V. Very well. Then I've been a middling, average, speckled, neither-better-nor-worse-than-my-neighbour sort of man. Does that satisfy you?

ALMA. No! No! Why do you torture me? Don't you see that I want to forgive you? My heart's aching to forgive you! Why won't you tell me the truth?

SIR V. (*very seriously*). I will. There are hundreds of things in my past life that I'm ashamed of. I hide them from you, I hide them from myself, not because I wish to deceive you, not because I wish you to think me white, when I'm — well, not black, but rather a darkish shade of whitey-brown. I hide them from you because I love you, and I don't wish to bring anything profane into your presence.

ALMA (*pleased*). Ah!

SIR V. Don't think that we men don't value such women as you. The best and purest woman in this world doesn't set a thousandth part of the value on herself that the man who loves her does. We know there are two kinds of women. And it's you, and not the others, that we will have at our firesides. It's you, and not the others, that we will have for our mothers, and sisters, and wives.

ALMA. But this woman——

SIR V. She's nothing to me. She has been nothing to me.

ALMA. Oh, don't tell me that—don't you see I want to forgive you? There never was a woman so weak and foolish as I am. I'm ready to forgive you anything, everything—only do give me some reasonable excuse. I want to look up to you. I want to worship you. I want to feel proud that you are my master. I will do it if you will only be perfectly truthful and frank with me. Oh, do earn all my love and faithfulness by not deceiving me! Say that you have been foolish with this woman—that you have been led away—deceived! say anything—put what colour you like on it—only don't tell me a falsehood about her. Be open with me.

SIR V. Give me your hand. Look at me. Look straight into my eyes. You shall believe me. She is nothing to me; she has been nothing to me. The moment you discovered us was the only moment when such a suspicion could have come to you. I was foolish. It was only for a moment.

ALMA. But these scandals about you and her?

SIR V. They are only scandals. There's not a breath of truth in them. You believe me?

ALMA. I must when you look at me like that.

SIR V. No; believe me because I'm speaking the truth.

ALMA. I do. I will.

SIR V. And you accept me, knowing that I've not been perfect — in fact, that I've been very far from it.

ALMA. Oh, but you are perfect — at least as perfect as I want you to be. I wouldn't have you changed a bit from what you are. There! Aren't we women silly?

SIR V. And you'll face the scandal and marry me? (*She hides her head against him.*) I didn't catch your answer?

ALMA. When you please.

SIR V. To-morrow?

ALMA. To-morrow.

(WHEELER *crosses* L. *to* R.)

SIR V. I must wire Fentiman to meet me, so that I can get all my affairs straight. Have you a telegram form?

(ALMA *goes to desk, gets telegram form.* SIR VALENTINE *sits down at table and writes message.* WHEELER *admits* POTE, L.)

WHEELER. Mr. Pote wishes to see Mr. Jorgan, ma'am.

POTE. Oh, if you please, I wish to see him quite alone. It's very important.

ALMA. Fetch Mr. Jorgan here.

(*Exit* WHEELER, R.)

POTE. Thank you very much. I'm sorry to intrude, but it's really important. (*Goes up to* SIR VALENTINE, *who is writing.*) Sir Valentine——

SIR V. (*very busy over his telegram*). Not now, Mr. Pote.

POTE. But I wish to speak to you.

SIR V. Not now. I like orphans — I'm very fond of orphans — but they really ought to be careful whom they employ to give them their bread and treacle. (*Rising, goes to* ALMA, *shows her the telegram.*) I'll send this off and be back in a few minutes.

ALMA (*in a low voice to him*). And I'll tell Lady Beauboys that I've discovered a perfect man.

SIR V. Don't make me out too perfect, in case——

ALMA. But you're going to be quite perfect in the future, aren't you?

SIR V. Oh, quite perfect — in the future.

(*Exit,* L.)

Enter JORGAN, R.

ALMA (*to* JORGAN). Mr. Pote wishes to see you.   (*Exit,* R.)

JOR. Well, Pote, what is it?

POTE (*very solemn and important*). Mr. Jorgan, I've made a very painful discovery.

JOR. (*ghastly*). No, Pote, no? Not about me?

POTE. Yes, Mr. Jorgan, about you.

JOR. (*collapses*). No, Pote! Impossible!

POTE. That's what I should have said six months ago, but unfortunately it's only too true.

JOR. What do you know?

POTE. You remember Eliza?

JOR. (*freshly alarmed*). Eliza? No! What Eliza?

POTE. My niece, Eliza Paddon. She stayed in Pewbury with me five years ago.

JOR. What if she did? What's that got to do with me?

POTE. She remembers you, though you don't remember her.

JOR. Well?

POTE. Three months ago I saw her in London, and she told me she had seen you a few days before in the company of a young woman in the Edgeware Road.

JOR. What was I doing?

POTE. You were looking into all the drapers' shop windows, and admiring the dresses. I told her at the time she was mistaken, because I thought she was.

JOR. So she was, Pote! So she was!

POTE (*shakes his head*). My suspicions have been aroused for some time past, especially by the large sum you subscribed to the widows' home three months ago.

Jor. There! There! If I hadn't been so conscientious you wouldn't have found me out. It's my goodness of heart in trying to make amends that has ruined me!

Pote (*continuing*). And when I witnessed your strange conduct with this person the day before yesterday, I wasn't at all satisfied, so I went up to London and I took a photograph of you with me.

Jor. What for?

Pote. For purposes of identification.

Jor. That was very underhanded of you, Pote.

Pote. We're obliged to be a little underhanded in the cause of morality sometimes. I took your photograph, and I went into all the drapers' shops in the neighbourhood, and I found out where you bought a red satin and a blue velvet dress. Oh, Mr. Jorgan! Oh, Mr. Jorgan!

Jor. (*nearly in tears*). That's what I say to myself, Pote, a hundred times a day. On thinking the matter over, I decline to believe that I could have been guilty. There must be some aberration somewhere!

Pote. Yes, in your conduct. Oh, Mr. Jorgan! Oh, Mr. Jorgan!

Jor. Does anybody suspect me — except yourself?

Pote. Not at present. Eliza didn't remember you sufficiently to be sure, and your eminent character leads her to suppose she was mistaken.

Jor. She must have been! It couldn't have been me.

Pote. Unfortunately, I've got the bill of the red satin and the blue velvet dress. Here's a copy of it. (*Giving him a copy.*)

Jor. (*takes it, looks at it*). Do the shop-people know who I am? (*Puts it in his pocket.*)

Pote. Not at present. But they recognised you immediately from your photograph.

Jor. You won't expose me, Pote?

Pote. I'm afraid I must in the interests of morality.

Jor. It can't be for the interests of morality for me to be exposed. Oh, Pote, you don't know what a moral lesson this has been for me — what an awful moral lesson!

Pote. I'm glad to hear it, Mr. Jorgan, and I wish I could see my way to spare you — honestly I do.

Jor. You will, Pote? You will? (*Crying.*) Remember what my position is!

Pote. Yes, you've always been such a professor, haven't you? That's a pity! You shouldn't have professed more than you were able to act up to.

JOR. I always thought I was able to act up to it. And I intend to for — the future. Do let things stay as they are!

POTE. But everybody thinks Sir Valentine is guilty——

JOR. Well, that won't matter to him so much. He has never professed to be so very moral, so his character won't suffer as mine will. Besides, if he isn't guilty of this, you may depend he's guilty of something quite as bad, if not worse. You won't expose me, Pote?

POTE. I really wish I could see my way to spare you. I want to do what is best for the interests of morality.

JOR. That's it — that's it! Don't make it a personal question. Let's see what will be best for the interests of morality. Don't speak loud, Pote! So many people are about. (*Goes anxiously to both doors to see that no one is looking.*) Now let's reckon up what will happen if I'm exposed. Morality in Market Pewbury will receive such a blow as it will never recover from, and then see what an effect it will have on our business. Although we do cut prices very fine, and our trade's increasing, yet you must remember that ours is a very moral connection, Pote; and if my misfortune is known, our trade will suffer for years.

POTE. Yes, that's true; but I don't think I ought to put business before morality.

JOR. Certainly not—certainly not! Let's put morality first. In spite of my misfortune, I assure you, Pote, there isn't any man more moral at heart than I am. Well, see the effect it will have on the character of the boot and shoe trade generally. It will distinctly lower our profession in the eyes of the world. And then the orphan asylum.

POTE. Yes, I forgot. The first lot of orphans arrived at Pewbury at the same time that I did.

JOR. Where are they?

POTE. Well, it wouldn't do for them to come on here whilst things are in this dreadful state, would it?

JOR. What have you done with them?

POTE. I sent them on to the schoolroom, and ordered them a bun each; and told them to sing some hymns for an hour or two.

JOR. Poor little dears! What's to become of them?

POTE. Ah, that's what I want to know! What is to become of them?

JOR. Don't speak so loud, Pote. (*Emphatically.*) They *must* come on here now. If you expose me the subscriptions will fall off, and the orphan asylum will go to smash. Don't stand in the way of four hundred and fifty little orphans, Pote. Don't ruin *their* prospects. Do let things stay as they are. Don't expose me.

POTE. Yes, but what about Sir Valentine's character?

JOR. Don't I keep on telling you that he has no special moral character to keep up like I have. Besides, how badly he treated you the other day. I felt quite indignant when I saw him pulling your ear.

POTE. Yes, he did pull my ear, and he was quite insulting to me just now. Still, I don't feel quite justified in——

JOR. Take my word, you are quite justified, Pote. (*Very imploringly.*) Say you'll let things stay as they are? Oh, Pote, it has been such a moral lesson to me! Quite a blessing in disguise! It will enable me to be *such* a warning and *such* a terror to evildoers in the future. Do keep quiet, and let us have a beautiful happy opening of our orphanage asylum. Do, Pote, do, in the interests of morality!

POTE (*after a little pause*). Well, perhaps, considering everything, it will be conducive to the interests of morality if I hold my tongue.

JOR. (*immensely grateful*). I'm sure it

ACT III THE TRIUMPH OF THE PHILISTINES 117

will — I'm sure it will! Then you'll let things stay as they are, eh, Pote?

SIR VALENTINE *enters carelessly,* L., *stands and looks at them. They show slight confusion.*

POTE. Yes, Mr. Jorgan, and I'll fetch the orphans at once.

JOR. (*again very cheerful and jubilant*). Do, Pote, do! And trust to me to bring everything to a glorious issue.

(POTE *looks at* SIR VALENTINE, *and sneaks off,* L. SIR VALENTINE *looks after him, comes to* JORGAN.)

SIR V. What confounded bit of rascality are you bringing to a glorious issue, eh? What's going on here? Eh? eh?

JOR. I'll give you a bit of friendly advice, Sir Valentine. You make haste and clear out of Market Pewbury before it gets too hot for you.

SIR V. Ah! How so?

JOR. Public feeling runs very high in England on questions of morality.

SIR V. (*suddenly enlightened*). You scoundrel! you hypocrite!

JOR. What now? What now?

SIR V. That woman is your accomplice! Own it! You've put her up to slander and blackmail me. Own it! Confess! (*Pause.*)

JOR. (*looking round uneasily*). If I confess, will you let me off, eh? If I persuade her to go off quiet, will you let me keep my character?

SIR V. No, I'll expose you. Come, own it, I say! (*A pause.*)

JOR. (*desperately*). I know nothing of her. Don't you try to palm her off on me. Don't you try to make me your scapegoat, it won't do. All the town knows your history.

SIR V. All the town shall know yours.

JOR. It does. Thank goodness, everybody in Market Pewbury knows my character. I think my word will be taken against yours. But if you don't think so, you try it on. Prove what you say!

SALLY (*appears at door*, R., *calls off*). Let be my luggages! Do you hear? Put down my luggages! (*Comes to* SIR VALENTINE.)

Re-enter LADY BEAUBOYS *and* ALMA, R.

SALLY. My Valentine! tell our footmens to come and take my luggages.

LADY B. (*speaking off*). Take them outside; put them on the carriage; drive to the station, and send them off to London by the express train, carriage paid.

SALLY (*looking round, sees* LADY BEAUBOYS'

ACT III THE TRIUMPH OF THE PHILISTINES 119

shawl, fan, and parasol lying on the chair where LADY BEAUBOYS *had previously left them, swoops down on them*). Ah!
(*Puts on the shawl, opens the parasol, fans herself with the fan.*)
LADY B. How dare you! How dare you!
SALLY. Ah! get away, Auntie Beauboys. You steal my luggages! Ver' well, I steal yours! How you like me now, my Valentine?
(*Fanning herself.*)

SKEWETT *enters*, L., *followed by* BLAGG, MODLIN, WAPES, *and* CORBY. *They all stand surprised and shocked, looking at* SALLY, *who stands fanning herself and twirling round the parasol.*

SALLY. Ah! how do you do? How you like this style all of you? Here, all you gentlemen! How you like me in Aunty Beauboys' rags what she stand upright in?
BLAGG. Are we in heathen Greece and Rome, or is this Market Pewbury?
MOD. Ain't these your premises now, Mr. Jorgan?
WAPES. Yes, Mr. Jorgan, this aint the sort of thing, you know, to set an example to the orphans.
SKEW. Turn her out! Make a clean sweep! Turn her out!

Sir V. I think Mr. Jorgan has a little explanation to make with regard to this young lady. Come, Mr. Jorgan, own up, if you please. Tell your friends all your pretty little story with this lady.

Jor. (*at bay, very desperately*). What do you think, gentlemen! You'll hardly believe it! Sir Valentine is actually trying to palm off his misdemeanour on me! Yes, gentlemen, he actually accuses me — me — of complicity with this female!

Sir V. (*to* Sally). Come! Tell the truth! This man has told you to accuse me so that you may get money from me. Do you hear! The truth! It is he who is guilty?

Sally. Oh no, my Valentine. You are the guilty party. You have compromised me. Now you must pay up like a gentleman.

(Jorgan *turns triumphantly to his comrades.*)

Sir V. (*stands for a moment or two very quietly, looks round contemptuously, shrugs his shoulders. Very long pause. To* Alma). Do you still believe me?

Alma. Yes.

Sir V. Are you ready to leave Market Pewbury at once?

Alma. Quite.

Sir V. Auntie, my carriage is outside. Will you come up to town with us?

LADY B. What for?

SIR V. Mrs. Suleny and I are to be married to-morrow morning, and we leave England to-morrow evening. We shall want you to see us through.

LADY B. Certainly, Valentine.

Enter POTE, L.

POTE. The orphans have arrived — they're waiting outside.

SIR V. (*genially*). Bring them in, Mr. Pote — bring them in! (*Takes out his cigar-case and selects a cigar very carefully, takes out match-box, and lights cigar with great nonchalance, during the following speech*). Gentlemen, I regret exceedingly that I've not been able to conform to the manners and morals of Market Pewbury. An ancient moralist, as you may remember, profoundly remarked that when you go to Market Pewbury you must do as Market Pewbury does. With all respect to you, I'll see Market Pewbury at — at Market Pewbury first. I had a comfortable little fifteen thousand a year which I should have been delighted to have spent amongst you in making you happy. But I regret to say I must keep that comfortable fifteen thousand a year in my pockets and spend it amongst your more genial neighbours on the Continent. (*A very sneering, contemptuous laugh from* JORGAN.) I leave you the dust from my feet, and my reputation to tear to pieces as you please. And I leave you this very charming couple, Mr. Jorgan and Mademoiselle Lebrune, to be the pillars of morality in your ancient borough. (JORGAN *laughs again. To* ALMA.) Are you ready?

ALMA. Quite.

SIR V. Now, auntie.

(LADY BEAUBOYS *and* ALMA *exeunt*, L.)

SIR V. (*cigar in mouth, looks at them a moment*). Good-day, gentlemen.

(*Exit.* JORGAN, *laughing triumphantly, watches him off.*)

SALLY. He is gone! (*springing on* JORGAN'S *neck.*) Ah! You are all I have in the world!

(JORGAN'S *face, ghastly with terror, is seen above* SALLY'S *arms, which are tightly clasped round his neck,* WAPES *and the others looking on, surprised.*)

CURTAIN.

www.ingramcontent.com/pod-product-compliance
Lightning Source LLC
LaVergne TN
LVHW091307080426
835510LV00007B/394